ACCESS TO 200+ SARASOTA RESTAURANT MENUS

The
Little Sarasota
DINING
Book.

dineSARASOTA

2026

OUR 17TH ANNUAL EDITION!

SARASOTA'S BEST SELLING RESTAURANT GUIDE

DINESARASOTA.COM

The Little Sarasota DINING Book.
17th Edition | 2026

dineSarasota

To contact us, please send email to:
press@dinesarasota.com

Printed in the USA

10 9 8 7 6 5 4 3 2 1

ISBN 979-8-9920516-1-2

THANK YOU!

Thanks for picking up the 17th edition of our annual Sarasota dining book. We are so happy to be able to provide you with Sarasota restaurant information that you can use every day!

These annual dining guides take some time to put together. It would be great if they wrote themselves, but sadly, they don't. The good news is we have help! And we are very thankful for it.

Thanks to Mila Aguiar, AJ Altes, Anna Denton, Dyann Hawkins, Mark Majorie, Steve Phelps, Joyce Pizzichillo, Raul Rodriguez, Anne Rollings, Broc Smith, and Eddie Zaki for contributing content to this year's edition. It is fantastic to have such talented people in our community. We are grateful that they have taken the time to provide content for this year's edition.

Cindi Kievit makes sure it's actually possible for you to read all the things we write about. Thank you for your editing skills and masterful use of the red pen.

As always, thanks to you! Thank you for supporting what we do. We're always striving to make sure that our local Sarasota restaurants get the attention they so richly deserve. I know that they appreciate you, too!

Here we are once again. I would say we have to stop meeting like this, but in all honesty, I love it! This marks the 17th edition of the *Little Sarasota DINING Book*. It is more than a little hard to imagine, really.

Last year, we wrote about recovery. For both our residents and our restaurant community. This year is all about growth. With the harsh reality of Helene and Milton fading just a bit, new restaurants are opening at a rate that we haven't seen since 2005.

Waterside, UTC, LWR, Wellen Park, and Rosemary are all sprouting new places to dine in and carry out. The rate at which places have been opening is eye-popping. We're certainly pulling for every new spot that opens its doors to serve our locals and visitors.

It seems like everything is more expensive these days. With that weekly or twice-weekly restaurant outing getting more costly, you'll need to make good dining choices. We'll do everything in our power to highlight the places that are getting it right.

Our *Sarasota Bites* newsletter is a good place for you to start gathering info. It's published weekly and will give you a little inside insight to help make those "where should we go tonight" decisions just a bit easier. Nearly 6,000 Sarasota foodies already subscribe. Maybe you should, too! (We're making it easy to sign up. There are QR codes sprinkled throughout this book for you to scan to subscribe!)

Thanks again for picking up #17 and for making dineSarasota part of your dining decision loop. We appreciate you.

Larry Hoffman
Publisher, dineSarasota.com

dS
dineSarasota

2026 DINESARASOTA TOP 50

- [ ] 1   Beso
- [ ] 2   Pazzo on Orange
- [ ] 3   The Shebeen Irish Pub & Kitchen
- [ ] 4   Mouthole Smashburgers
- [ ] 5   Tony's Chicago Beef
- [ ] 6   The DUO Döner & Deli
- [ ] 7   Summer House Steak & Seafood
- [ ] 8   Indigenous
- [ ] 9   Michael's on East
- [ ] 10   Walt's Fish Market & Restaurant
- [ ] 11   La Violetta
- [ ] 12   Lucky 8 *
- [ ] 13   Hive Bar
- [ ] 14   Captain Brian's
- [ ] 15   Vino Vino
- [ ] 16   Samba Brazilian Steakhouse *
- [ ] 17   Lefty's Oyster & Seafood Bar *
- [ ] 18   Millie's Café
- [ ] 19   Rosemary and Thyme
- [ ] 20   GROVE Restaurant
- [ ] 21   Island House Tap & Grill
- [ ] 22   Connors Steak & Seafood
- [ ] 23   Double Deez Chicago Hot Dogs
- [ ] 24   Drift Kitchen and Bar
- [ ] 25   Ringside (Cirque St. Armands) *
- [ ] 26   Lenny'z Pizza & Island Bar
- [ ] 27   Florence and the Spice Boys
- [ ] 28   Naked Farmer
- [ ] 29   The Cottage

☐	30	Osteria 500
☐	31	Capo Pazzo
☐	32	Big Water Fish Market
☐	33	131 Main *
☐	34	Cuba 1958
☐	35	The Fat Rabbit
☐	36	Wolfie Cohen's Rascal House
☐	37	Pacific Rim
☐	38	Mattison's Forty One
☐	39	Miguel's
☐	40	Brine Seafood & Raw Bar
☐	41	Casey Key Fish House
☐	42	Fork & Hen
☐	43	Spice Station
☐	44	Arts & Central
☐	45	The Mable
☐	46	Karl Ehmer's Alpine Steak House
☐	47	The Village Café
☐	48	Clasico Italian Chophouse
☐	49	Divan
☐	50	Malmosto Wine Shop & Kitchen

Opened since our last edition.

HOW TO USE THIS CHECKLIST - Like you really need an explanation for this. But, just in case, here goes. Get out there and eat through our Top 50! We've made it easy for you to keep track of your culinary adventures. These are the restaurants that you've been searching for, clicking on, and downloading on our dineSarasota.com website all year. So, in a way, this is really *your* Top 50. And, if you flip to the back of this book, we've left a couple of note pages for you to keep track of your favorites. Go ahead, start your own Sarasota restaurant journal.

HOW TO USE THIS BOOK

Thanks for picking up a copy of the latest *Little Sarasota DINING Book*. We're hoping that you're going to use it as your go-to guide to Sarasota dining. Now that you're the proud owner of a copy, we're going to give you some helpful inside tips on how to use the guide.

First off, it's arranged alphabetically. So, if you know the alphabet, you can use our guide. Yes, it's really that easy. It has basic restaurant information in each listing. Name, address, phone… it also lists the restaurant's website if you would like to go there for additional information.

In the outlined bar, it will tell you the neighborhood/area where the restaurant is located, the cuisine it serves, and its relative expense. It's relative to Sarasota, not NYC; keep that in mind.

We list the hours of operation for each restaurant. It helps to know when they are open. We try our best to make this info as accurate as possible. But sometimes, Sarasota restaurants have special seasonal hours. We apologize in advance if a place may have changed their hours after we went to print. If there's a question, it's always best to call the restaurant.

For each place we'll also tell you what you can expect. Is it noisy or quiet? Good for kids? Maybe a late night menu. It's not an exhaustive list, just some of the highlights to guide your dining decision-making process.

We'll give you a few Best Bites. It's a quick look at what's on the menu. Again, we try our best to keep these current, but…

There aren't a lot of mysterious symbols that you have to reference. If you see this *, it means the restaurant has more than one location. We've listed what we consider to be the main one. The other locations are usually listed in the super handy cross reference in the back of the book.

Speaking of the cross reference, here's the scoop. Restaurants are listed in alphabetical order (you're good at that now!). We give you basic info: Name, address, phone. Restaurants are then listed by cuisine type and then by location. So, you can easily find that perfect seafood restaurant on Longboat Key.

QR CODES. Each restaurant listing has a little square box with a bunch of jumbled up dots. That's your easy access to the menu for that restaurant. Just scan that little code with the QR reader or camera on your smartphone and, just like magic, there's the menu! Pretty great, right? Oh, what if I don't have a smartphone? Well, then it just might be time...

SPECIALTY CATEGORIES. OK. Here's where things really get interesting. You now know where things are located and what type of food you can expect. But, let's dive in a little deeper. Let's say you're just visiting beautiful, sunny Sarasota AND you've got kids. What would be a good choice? How about celebrating a special occasion or event? Or, maybe you would just like to eat a meal and enjoy a spectacular water view. Where's the best spot?

That's where our specialty categories come in. Here are some things to keep in mind. First, we've curated these restaurant lists just for you. Second, these places may not be the only ones in town that fit the description. But, we think they're among the best. Hey, why isn't my favorite pizza place on that list? We're not trying to snub anybody here, but there's only so much space.

LIVE MUSIC – Really self-explanatory. But, the music ranges from piano bar to acoustic guitar to rock 'n' roll. So, you may want to see who's playing the night you're going. Also, yes, there are other places in town that have live music.

CATERING – You could probably convince most restaurants to cater your twelve person dinner or throw together some to-go food for you to arrange on your own platters. The places listed here do it for REAL. They cater regularly.

EASY ON YOUR WALLET – A little perspective is in order here. Nothing on this list comes close to the McDonald's Dollar Menu (thankfully). That being said, these are some places you could go and not have to sell some jewelry to pay the tab. Something to keep in mind, "Easy on the wallet" depends a little on how big your billfold is. These restaurants won't break the budget.

NEW – No explanation necessary. These restaurants are "relatively" new. Some have been open longer than others. But, they've opened since our last edition.

SPORTS + FOOD + FUN – The big game is on and you want to see it. Here are some places that do that well. Lots of places have a TV in the bar. These go above and beyond that.

GREAT BURGERS – For the past year, our *A Burger A Week* series has been running in our newsletter, *Sarasota Bites*. We'll give you some of the highlights in this burger listing.

NICE WINE LIST – Hmmm… A 2006 Cabernet or a 2015 Pouilly-Fuissé? That is one tough question. No "wine in a box" here. These restaurants all have a sturdy wine list and are proud of it. Sometimes it can certainly be a little intimidating choosing a wine. These spots usually have someone to hold your hand and walk you through it.

A BEAUTIFUL WATER VIEW – Nothing says Florida like a picture perfect view of the water. And, these places have that. The food runs the gamut from bar food to fine dining.

LATER NIGHT MENU – This is not New York, and it is not Miami or Chicago either. That is the context with which you should navigate this list. Notice we said "LATER" night menu and NOT "late night menu." We're a reasonably early dining town. The places listed here are open past the time when half of Sarasota is safely tucked in bed. They might not all be 1AM, but we do have a few choices if you're still out past 2am!

SARASOTA FINE DINING – It's not great when people look down their noses at our upscale dining scene. We have some damn good chefs here in Sarasota. And, they're showing off their skills every single day. They should be celebrated. This list may not contain Le Bernardin, Alinea, or The French Laundry. But, we have some REAL contenders.

Lastly, there is always the question, "How do these restaurants get into this book?" They are selected based on their yearly popularity on dineSarasota.com. These are the restaurants that YOU are interested in. You've been searching for them on our website all year long. There are no advertisements here. So, you can't "buy your way in." It's all you. This is really YOUR guide. And, I must say, you have great taste!

ALMA DE ESPAÑA

NEW

1830 South Osprey Avenue
941-365-8426
almatapasandgrill.com

SOUTHSIDE VILLAGE	SPANISH	COST: $$$

HOURS: Daily, 5PM to 10PM

WHAT TO EXPECT: Nice Wine List • Casual Spanish Tapas
Indoor & Outdoor Seating • Great Desserts

BEST BITES: Ostras al Azafran • Croquetas de Jamon
Paella de Madrid • Flan de Chocolate y Ron

SCAN FOR MENU

SOME BASICS

Reservations:	YES
Spirits:	BEER/WINE
Parking:	LOT/STREET
Outdoor Dining:	YES

ALPINE STEAKHOUSE & BUTCHER SHOP

4520 South Tamiami Trail
941-922-3797
alpinesteak.com

SOUTH TRAIL	AMERICAN	COST: $$

HOURS: Tue to Sat, 9AM to 9PM
CLOSED SUNDAY & MONDAY

WHAT TO EXPECT: Great Butcher Shop • Home Of The "TurDuckHen"
German Cuisine • Featured On The Food Network

BEST BITES: TurDuckHen • Steaks! • ½ lb Sirloin Burger
German Sausage Sampler • Texas Baby Back Ribs

SCAN FOR MENU

SOME BASICS

Reservations:	NO
Spirits:	FULL BAR
Parking:	LOT
Outdoor Dining:	NO

AMORE RESTAURANT
180 North Lime Avenue
941-383-1111
amorelbk.com

COLONIAL VILLAGE	ITALIAN	COST: $$$

HOURS: Wed-Sun, 5PM to 9PM
CLOSED MONDAY & TUESDAY

WHAT TO EXPECT: OpenTable Reservations • Upscale Italian Cuisine
Casual, Relaxed Atmosphere • Also A Portuguese Menu

BEST BITES: Pica-Pua de Vaca • Bacalhau Ribatenjo
Chicken Livornese • Salmon Picatta • Beef Osso Bucco

SCAN FOR MENU

SOME BASICS
Reservations:	YES
Spirits:	BEER/WINE
Parking:	LOT
Outdoor Dining:	NO

ANDREA'S
2085 Siesta Drive
941-951-9200
andreasrestaurantsrq.com

SOUTHGATE	ITALIAN	COST: $$$

HOURS: Mon-Sat, 5PM to 10PM
CLOSED SUNDAY (summer only)

WHAT TO EXPECT: Nice Wine List • Quiet Restaurant Atmosphere
Upscale Italian Cuisine • Great Special Occasion Place

BEST BITES: Polenta Concia • Tonnarelli Sunday Style
Veal Tripe Piemontese • Short Ribs Andreas

SCAN FOR MENU

SOME BASICS
Reservations:	YES
Spirits:	BEER/WINE
Parking:	LOT
Outdoor Dining:	NO

ANNA MARIA OYSTER BAR

6906 14th Street W.*
941-758-7880
oysterbar.net

BRADENTON	SEAFOOD	COST: $$

HOURS: Sun-Thur, 11AM to 9PM
Fri-Sat, 11AM to 10PM

WHAT TO EXPECT: Good For Kids • Casual, Family Atmosphere
Large Menu • Good For Groups

BEST BITES: Lots Of Raw Bar Options • Mussels Provencal
Conch Fritters • Pier Poke Bowl • Linguine With Scallops
Lobster Bisque • Gulf Grouper Sandwich • Live ME Lobster

SOME BASICS

SCAN FOR MENU

Reservations:	8 OR MORE
Spirits:	FULL BAR
Parking:	LOT
Outdoor Dining:	YES

ANNA'S DELI & SANDWICH SHOP

6535 Midnight Pass Road*
941-349-4888
annasdelis.com

SIESTA KEY	DELI	COST: $

HOURS: Daily, 10:30AM to 4PM

WHAT TO EXPECT: Super Casual • Great Sandwiches (The Surfer)
Good For SK Beach To Go • Super Fast Service

BEST BITES: Sandwiches Are What They Do! • Surfer
Peddler • Villager • Skater • Fiesta

SOME BASICS

SCAN FOR MENU

Reservations:	NO
Spirits:	NONE
Parking:	LOT
Outdoor Dining:	NO

APOLLONIA GRILL

8235 Cooper Creek Boulevard*
941-359-4816
apolloniagrill.com

UPARK	GREEK	COST: $$

HOURS: Mon-Thur, 11:30AM to 9PM • Fri & Sat, 11:30AM to 10PM
Sunday, 11:30AM to 8:30PM

WHAT TO EXPECT: Good For Groups • Family Owned
Casual Dining • Lots Of Parking • Also A Landings Location

BEST BITES: Avegolemono Soup • Lamb Shank Osso Bucco
Seafood Salad • Spinach & Feta Flatbread • Moussaka

SCAN FOR MENU

SOME BASICS

Reservations:	YES
Spirits:	FULL BAR
Parking:	LOT
Outdoor Dining:	YES

ARTS & CENTRAL

611 Central Avenue
941-306-2356
artsandcentral.com

ROSEMARY DIST	AMERICAN	COST: $$$

HOURS: Sun-Thur, 11AM to 11PM • Fri & Sat, 11AM to 12AM
Sunday Brunch, 11AM to 4PM

WHAT TO EXPECT: Big Dining Room • Can Be Noisy Inside
Great Outdoor Dining Space • Live Music ♫

BEST BITES: Lamb Sliders • Whipped Feta • 611 Salad
Pork Belly & Octopus • Grilled Trout • Backyard Bahn Mi

SCAN FOR MENU

SOME BASICS

Reservations:	YES
Spirits:	FULL BAR
Parking:	STREET
Outdoor Dining:	YES

ATHENS FAMILY RESTAURANT
2300 Bee Ridge Road
941-706-4121
athensfamilyrestaurant.business.site

THE COLONNADE	GREEK	COST: $$

HOURS: Mon-Sat, 8AM to 10PM
CLOSED SUNDAY

WHAT TO EXPECT: Casual Greek Cuisine • Good For Families
Family Owned & Operated • Lots Of Parking

BEST BITES: Greek Omelet • Bakaliaro Sandwich
Horiatiki Salad • Bifteki Platter • Baklava

SOME BASICS
Reservations: NO
Spirits: BEER/WINE
Parking: LOT
Outdoor Dining: NO

SCAN FOR MENU

ATRIA BREAD + COFFEE
4120 Lakewood Ranch Boulevard
941-751-1016
atria.cafe

LAKEWOOD RANCH	AMERICAN	COST: $$

HOURS: Café Open Daily, 8AM to 2:30PM
Pizza, Tue-Sat, 5PM to 8PM

WHAT TO EXPECT: Café By Day - Pizza By Night! • Specialty Coffee
Catering Available

BEST BITES: Hokkaido Milk Bread • Cherries Jubilee French Toast
Umami Eggs Benedict • Crispy Chicken Sandwich
Pizza • Pumpkin Madeleine

SOME BASICS
Reservations: NO
Spirits: NONE
Parking: LOT
Outdoor Dining: YES

SCAN FOR MENU

BAKER AND WIFE
2157 Siesta Drive
941-960-1765
bakerwife.com

SOUTHGATE	AMERICAN	COST: $$

HOURS: Thur-Sat, 5PM to 9PM

WHAT TO EXPECT: Artisan Pizza • Casual Atmosphere
Lots Of Dessert Choices • OpenTable Reservations

BEST BITES: Beef Carpaccio • Spicy Tuna Tartare • Caesar Salad
Pan Seared Salmon • Buckhead Beef Grilled Skirt Steak
The Meatball • Pizza! • Double Bacon Cheeseburger

SCAN FOR MENU

SOME BASICS
Reservations:	YES
Spirits:	FULL BAR
Parking:	LOT
Outdoor Dining:	YES

BANGKOK RESTAURANT
4791 Swift Road
941-922-0703
bangkoksrq.com

	THAI	COST: $$

HOURS: Lunch - Mon-Fri, 11:30AM to 2PM
Dinner - Daily 5PM

WHAT TO EXPECT: Casual Thai Cuisine • Lots Of Parking
One Of Sarasota's Oldest Thai Restaurants

BEST BITES: Thai-Yai Ribs • Tom Yum • Lap Gai
Bangkok Cashew Nut • Massamann Curry
Pad Woon Sen • Seafood Ladnar • Thai Crispy

SCAN FOR MENU

SOME BASICS
Reservations:	YES
Spirits:	BEER/WINE
Parking:	LOT
Outdoor Dining:	NO

BAR HANA
1289 North Palm Avenue
941-536-9717
barhana.com

DOWNTOWN	ASIAN	COST: $$$

HOURS: Sun-Thur, 11AM to 12M
Fri & Sat, 11AM to 2AM

WHAT TO EXPECT: Fantastic Craft Cocktails • Upscale Atmosphere
They Serve The Kojo Menu After 5P

BEST BITES: Siesta Key Swizzle • Frisky Flamingo • Sashimi
Crispy Nori Tacos • Grilled Wagyu Steak Lettuce Wraps
Bao Buns • Florida Rock Shrimp Tempura

SOME BASICS
SCAN FOR MENU

Reservations:	YES
Spirits:	FUL BAR
Parking:	STREET/GARAGE
Outdoor Dining:	YES

THE BARNYARD
620 Martin Luther King Ave W.
941-896-8760
barnyardbetty.com

BRADENTON	AMERICAN	COST: $$

HOURS: Mon-Sat, 11AM to 9PM

WHAT TO EXPECT: Casual • Great For Families • Burgers & More
Catering Available • Family Owned-Operated

BEST BITES: The Original Barnyard Betty! • Smash Burger Basket
Wings! • Double Crunch Fries

SOME BASICS
SCAN FOR MENU

Reservations:	NONE
Spirits:	NONE
Parking:	LOT
Outdoor Dining:	NO

BEACH HOUSE WATERFRONT RESTAURANT
200 Gulf Drive North
941-779-2222
beachhousedining.com

BRADENTON BEACH	AMERICAN	COST: $$

HOURS: Daily, 11:30AM to 10PM

WHAT TO EXPECT: Great For A Date • Florida Seafood
Nice Wine List • Lots Of Outdoor Dining Space

BEST BITES: House Smoked Fish-Dip • Gamble Farm House Salad
Seafood Gumbo • Short Rib Tacos • Key Lime Pie

SCAN FOR MENU

SOME BASICS

Reservations:	NO
Spirits:	FULL BAR
Parking:	LOT
Outdoor Dining:	YES

BEAN COFFEEHOUSE
5138 Ocean Boulevard
941-260-6400
beancoffeehouse.net

SIESTA KEY	AMERICAN	COST: $

HOURS: Daily, 7AM to 2PM

WHAT TO EXPECT: Great For A Date • Relaxed SK Coffee Shop
Basic Coffee Is Self Serve • Locals Gather Here!

BEST BITES: Coffee! • Fantastic Homemade Bialys! • Fruit Smoothies
Homemade Scones • Organic Wheat Toast Sandwiches
Hot & Iced Lattes • Egg Muffin Sandwiches

SCAN FOR INFO

SOME BASICS

Reservations:	NO
Spirits:	NONE
Parking:	LOT
Outdoor Dining:	YES

BESO

30 South Lemon Avenue
941-279-2999
besosrq.com

DOWNTOWN	SPANISH	COST: $$$

HOURS: Wed-Thur, 4PM to 10PM • Fri, 4PM to 11PM
Sat, 1PM to 11PM • Sun, 1PM to 10PM • CLOSED MON & TUE

WHAT TO EXPECT: Tapas Style Dining • Great Downtown Location
Great For Groups • Vibrant & Lively Atmosphere

BEST BITES: Queso de Cabra • Pintxos Mixtos • Charcuterie
Paella • Carillada de Ternera • Pollo Ajillo • Higos
Calamares • Trucha Escabeche • Flan • Basque Cheesecake

SOME BASICS

SCAN FOR MENU

Reservations:	YES
Spirits:	FULL BAR
Parking:	STREET/GARAGE
Outdoor Dining:	NO

BIG WATER FISH MARKET

6641 Midnight Pass Road
941-554-8101
bigwaterfishmarket.com

SIESTA KEY	SEAFOOD	COST: $$

HOURS: Mon-Sat, 11AM to 9PM
Sunday, 12PM to 8PM

WHAT TO EXPECT: Fresh Fish Market • Casual Dining
SK South Bridge Location • Key Lime Pie!

BEST BITES: Conch Cakes • "Jacks" Fish Stew • Hogfish
Grouper Reuben • Stone Crab (In Season) • Key Lime Pie

SOME BASICS

SCAN FOR MENU

Reservations:	NO
Spirits:	BEER/WINE
Parking:	LOT
Outdoor Dining:	NO

BLU KOUZINA

25 North Boulevard of the Presidents
941-388-2619
blukouzina.com/restaurants/sarasota

ST ARMANDS	GREEK	COST: $$$

HOURS: Mon-Thur, 4:30PM to 8:30PM
Fri-Sun, 11:30AM to 9:30PM

WHAT TO EXPECT: Upscale Greek Cuisine • St. Armands Circle
Parking Garage • Vibrant Atmosphere

INSIDER TIP: Lamb Shank (Lemonato) • "Santorini" Branzino
Lamb Ribs • Fasolosalata • Saganaki With Figs
Chicken Kalamaki

SCAN FOR MENU

SOME BASICS

Reservations:	YES
Spirits:	FULL BAR
Parking:	STREET/GARAGE
Outdoor Dining:	YES

BLUE DOLPHIN CAFÉ

470 John Ringling Boulevard
941-388-3566
bluedolphincafe.com

ST ARMANDS	AMERICAN	COST: $$

HOURS: Daily, 7AM to 2PM

WHAT TO EXPECT: Casual "Diner Style" • Breakfast & Lunch Only
Local Spot • Walk The Circle After Lunch!

INSIDER TIP: Breakfast Wrap • Homemade Corned Beef Hash
Gazpacho Daily • Surfer Burger • Chicken Salad Platter
Rachel Sandwich • Jet's Jewel Of A Sandwich!

SCAN FOR MENU

SOME BASICS

Reservations:	NO
Spirits:	NONE
Parking:	STREET/LOT
Outdoor Dining:	NO

BLVD CAFÉ

1580 Boulevard of the Arts
941-203-8102
blvdcafesrq.com

ROSEMARY DIST	AMERICAN	COST: $$

HOURS: Wed-Mon, 7AM to 5PM
CLOSED TUESDAY

WHAT TO EXPECT: Super Casual • Breakfast & Lunch Only
Lots Of Parking • Great Sidewalk Seating

INSIDER TIP: Braided Brioche French Toast • French Onion Soup
Seared Yellowfin Tuna Salad • Croque Monsieur
Salmon Bagel • Masala Chai Tea

SCAN FOR MENU

SOME BASICS

Reservations:	NO
Spirits:	NONE
Parking:	STREET
Outdoor Dining:	YES

BOCA SARASOTA

19 South Lemon Avenue
941-256-3565
bocasarasota.com

DOWNTOWN	AMERICAN	COST: $$

HOURS: Mon-Fri, 11AM to 10PM • Sat, 10AM to 11PM
Sun, 10AM to 10PM

WHAT TO EXPECT: Sat & Sun Brunch • Online Reservations
Classic Cocktails • Craft Beer Selections

BEST BITES: Skirt Steak • 60 Spiced Chicken • OMG Burger
Smoked Fish Dip • Flatbreads! • Grilled Caesar
Chopped Salad • Guava Cheesecake • Key Lime Jar

SCAN FOR MENU

SOME BASICS

Reservations:	YES
Spirits:	FULL BAR
Parking:	STREET
Outdoor Dining:	YES

THE BREAKFAST COMPANY

7246 55th Avenue E.*
941-201-6002
thebreakfastcompanyfl.com

BRADENTON	AMERICAN	COST: $$

HOURS: Tues-Sun, 7AM to 2PM
CLOSED MONDAY

WHAT TO EXPECT: Breakfast & Lunch Only • Local Ingredients
Good For Families • Also A Great Landings Location!

BEST BITES: Large Omelet Selection • Skillet Bowls
Terri's Famous Quiche • Strawberry Nutella French Toast
Scratch-Made Soups • California Cobb Salad

SCAN FOR MENU

SOME BASICS
Reservations:	NO
Spirits:	NONE
Parking:	LOT
Outdoor Dining:	YES

THE BREAKFAST HOUSE

1817 Fruitville Road
941-366-6860
sarasotabreakfasthouse.com

DOWNTOWN	AMERICAN	COST: $$

HOURS: Wed-Sun, 8AM to 2PM
CLOSED MONDAY & TUESDAY

WHAT TO EXPECT: Charming Atmosphere • Breakfast & Lunch
Great Omelets • Eclectic

BEST BITES: Lots Of Omelet Selections • Belgian Waffles
Lavender Stuffed Blueberry Pancakes • Vegan Skillet

SCAN FOR INFO

SOME BASICS
Reservations:	NO
Spirits:	NONE
Parking:	LOT
Outdoor Dining:	YES

BRICK'S SMOKED MEATS

1528 State Street
941-993-1435
brickssmokedmeats.com

DOWNTOWN	BBQ	COST: $$

HOURS: Sun-Thur, 11AM to 10PM • Friday, 11AM to 11PM
Saturday, 10AM to 1PM

WHAT TO EXPECT: State Street Garage • Bbq, Bbq, Bbq
Good Local Beer List • Great For A Group • Catering

BEST BITES: Pulled Pork • USDA Prime Brisket • St. Louis Ribs
Chicken Fried Chicken • Smoked Wings • Brisket Chili
Bacon Burnt Ends Tacos • State Street Corn

SCAN FOR MENU

SOME BASICS

Reservations:	NO
Spirits:	FULL BAR
Parking:	STREET/GARAGE
Outdoor Dining:	YES

BRINE SEAFOOD & RAW BAR

2250 Gulf Gate Drive
941-404-5639
BrineSarasota.com

GULF GATE	SEAFOOD	COST: $$

HOURS: Sun-Thur, 11AM to 10PM
Fri & Sat, 11AM to 11PM

WHAT TO EXPECT: Raw Bar • Northeastern Style Seafood
Busy During Season • Vibrant Atmosphere

BEST BITES: Oysters on the Half Shell • Charred Octopus
Cream Of Crab Soup • Jumbo Lump Crab Cakes
Pan Seared Snapper • Lobster Roll • Crab Cake Sandwich

SCAN FOR MENU

SOME BASICS

Reservations:	YES
Spirits:	FULL BAR
Parking:	LOT/STREET
Outdoor Dining:	YES

BULGOGI HOUSE

NEW

1472 Main Street
941-559-5678
bulgogihousefl.com

DOWNTOWN	KOREAN	COST: $$

HOURS: Lunch & Dinner Daily

WHAT TO EXPECT: Korean BBQ! • Fun For A Group
All You Can Eat Specials • Also Kitchen Cooked Dishes

BEST BITES: Beef Brisket • Beef Belly • LA Galbi
Fresh Pork Belly • Marinated Pork Shoulder
Cheese Corn • Bibimbap • Fresh Salmon

SCAN FOR MENU

SOME BASICS
Reservations:	YES
Spirits:	BEER/WINE
Parking:	STREET/GARAGE
Outdoor Dining:	NO

BUSHIDO SUSHI SRQ

3688 Webber Steet
941-217-5635
bushidosushisrq.com

	SUSHI	COST: $$

HOURS: Mon-Sat, 4PM to 9PM
CLOSED SUNDAY

WHAT TO EXPECT: Japanese Cuisine • Sushi • Casual Atmosphere
Good For Families

BEST BITES: Spicy Seafood Miso Soup • Hawaii Martini
Sashimi & Nigiri • Bushido Signature Rolls!
Teryiaki & Tempura Dishes

SCAN FOR MENU

SOME BASICS
Reservations:	YES
Spirits:	BEER & WINE
Parking:	LOT
Outdoor Dining:	NO

CAFÉ BARBOSSO
5501 Palmer Crossing Circle
941-922-7999
cafebarbosso.com

PALMER CROSSING	ITALIAN	COST: $$

HOURS: Tues-Sun, 4PM to 9PM
CLOSED MONDAY

WHAT TO EXPECT: Authentic NYC Italian • Casual Dining
Fun Dining Experience • Good For Groups

BEST BITES: Mozzarella in Carrozza • Fresh Mozzarella Caprese
Grandma's Spaghettini 'n Meatballs • Seafood Fra Diavolo
Chicken Marsala Or Piccata • Personal Pizzas!

SOME BASICS
Reservations:	YES
Spirits:	FULL BAR
Parking:	LOT
Outdoor Dining:	YES

SCAN FOR MENU

CAFÉ EPICURE
1298 North Palm Avenue
941-366-5648
cafeepicure.com

DOWNTOWN	ITALIAN	COST: $$

HOURS: Daily, 11:45AM to 10:30PM

WHAT TO EXPECT: Great For A Date • Wood Fired Pizza
Casual Italian Fare • Palm Avenue Garage

BEST BITES: Salumeria - Formaggi & Salumi • Tartare Di Tonni
Pappardelle Bolognese • Pasta E Fagioli
Milanese Di Pollo • Pizza • Filetto Di Salmone

SOME BASICS
Reservations:	YES
Spirits:	FULL BAR
Parking:	STREET/PALM GARAGE
Outdoor Dining:	YES

SCAN FOR MENU

CAFÉ GABBIANO

5104 Ocean Boulevard
941-349-1423
cafegabbiano.com

SIESTA KEY	ITALIAN	COST: $$$

HOURS: Daily, 5PM to 10PM

WHAT TO EXPECT: Great Wine List • Siesta Village Location
Lots Of Parking • OpenTable Reservations • Nightly Specials

BEST BITES: Formaggi & Salumi Plate • Bruschetta Di Ischia
The Poached Pear • Costolette Di Vitello • Ossobuco Ravioli
Branzino • Lasagne Bolognese

SCAN FOR MENU

SOME BASICS

Reservations:	YES
Spirits:	FULL BAR
Parking:	LOT
Outdoor Dining:	YES

CAFÉ ON ST. ARMANDS   `NEW`

431 St. Armands Circle
941-388-4415
cafeonstarmands.com

ST ARMANDS	MEDITERRANEAN	COST: $$$

HOURS: Daily, 10PM to 9PM

WHAT TO EXPECT: Nice Wine List • European Street-Side Dining
Newly Renovated (2025) • Nice Lunch Meetup Spot

BEST BITES: Quiche Lorraine • The Apollo Pita • Kefta
Croque Madame • Lobstercargot • Deviled Eggs
Grouper Toastie • Moroccan Crispy Duck

SCAN FOR MENU

SOME BASICS

Reservations:	YES
Spirits:	FULL BAR
Parking:	STREET/GARAGE
Outdoor Dining:	YES

CAPO PAZZO

2053 Reynolds Street
941-487-8677
capopazzo.com

SOUTH TRAIL	ITALIAN	COST: $$

HOURS: Mon, Wed, Thur, Sun, 11AM to 9PM
Fri & Sat, 11AM to 10PM • CLOSED TUESDAY

WHAT TO EXPECT: Casual Italian Cuisine • Good For Families
Fantastic NY Style Pizza!!

BEST BITES: Red & White Pizza Styles • Baked Ziti Bites • Farro Salad
Arancini • Potato Gnocchi • Penne Alla Vodka
Capo Garlic Knots

SOME BASICS

SCAN FOR MENU

Reservations:	YES
Spirits:	BEER & WINE
Parking:	LOT
Outdoor Dining:	NO

CAPTAIN CURT'S CRAB & OYSTER BAR

1200 Old Stickney Point Road
941-349-3885
captaincurts.com

SIESTA KEY	SEAFOOD	COST: $$

HOURS: Daily, 11AM to 2AM

WHAT TO EXPECT: Good For Kids • Super Casual • Lots Of Seafood
Ohio State Football HQ • Live Music • "Sniki Tiki"

BEST BITES: Award Winning Clam Chowder • Grouper Sandwich
Snow Crab Platter • Buffalo Wings! • Stone Crab (In Season)
Alaskan Fish And Chips • Crab Cake Sandwich

SOME BASICS

SCAN FOR MENU

Reservations:	NO
Spirits:	FULL BAR
Parking:	LOT
Outdoor Dining:	YES

CASA MASA

4862 South Tamiami Trail*
941-921-0578
casamasa-srq.com

LANDINGS	MEXICAN	COST: $$

HOURS: Daily, 11AM to 10PM

WHAT TO EXPECT: Tacos! • Casual Mexican Cuisine
Blue Corn Tortillas • New Siesta Key Location (2025)

BEST BITES: Salmon Scallop Crudo • Lobster Esquites • Batata
Queso & Chips Barbacoa De Lengua • Pork Al Pastor
Enmoladas De Pollo • Burritos & Quesadillas

SCAN FOR MENU

SOME BASICS

Reservations:	NO
Spirits:	FULL BAR
Parking:	LOT
Outdoor Dining:	NO

CASEY KEY FISH HOUSE

801 Blackburn Point Road
941-966-1901
caseykeyfishhouse.com

OSPREY	SEAFOOD	COST: $$

HOURS: Daily, 11:30AM to 9PM

WHAT TO EXPECT: Vacation Atmosphere • Local Seafood
Boat Docks • An "Old Florida" Feel • Live Music

BEST BITES: U Peel U Eat Shrimp • New England Clam Chowder
Grouper Sandwich • Shrimp Scampi • Seafood Pasta
Diver Scallops With Citrus Sauce • Key Lime Pie

SCAN FOR MENU

SOME BASICS

Reservations:	NO
Spirits:	FULL BAR
Parking:	LOT
Outdoor Dining:	YES

CASK & ALE
1548 Main Street
941-702-8740
caskalekitchen.com

DOWNTOWN	AMERICAN	COST: $$

HOURS: Mon-Fri, 3M to 2AM
Sat & Sun, 11AM to 2AM • Brunch 11AM to 2PM

WHAT TO EXPECT: Weekend Brunch • Daily Happy Hour
Craft Cocktails • Lively Atmosphere • Live Music

BEST BITES: House-Made Hummus • Spicy Asian Pork Wings
Flaming Nachos • Philly Cheese Steak Flatbread
Wedgie Salad • Damn Good Chicken Sandwich

SCAN FOR MENU

SOME BASICS
Reservations:	NO
Spirits:	FULL BAR
Parking:	STREET
Outdoor Dining:	YES

C'EST LA VIE!
1553 Main Street
941-906-9575
cestlaviesarasota.com

DOWNTOWN	FRENCH	COST: $$

HOURS: Mon-Wed, 7:30AM to 6PM • Thur-Sat, 7:30AM to 10PM
Sunday, 8:30AM to 5PM

WHAT TO EXPECT: Outdoor Tables • Relaxed Café Dining
Fantastic Bakery • OpenTable Reservations

BEST BITES: Le Petit Déjeuner • Chocolate Croissant • Crepes
Baguette Sandwiches • Omelets • Quiche Lorraine
Croq' Madame • Parisienne Salad

SCAN FOR MENU

SOME BASICS
Reservations:	YES
Spirits:	BEER/WINE
Parking:	STREET
Outdoor Dining:	YES

CHÂTEAU 13

535 13th Street W.
941-226-0110
chateau-13.com

BRADENTON	FRENCH	COST: $$$

HOURS: Dinner -Tue-Thur (last seating 8:30PM)
Dinner - Fri & Sat (last seating 9PM) • CLOSED SUN & MON

WHAT TO EXPECT: European Cuisine • Adult Dining Experience
Reservations Recommended • Nice Beer List

BEST BITES: Beef Tartare • Escargots à la Bourguignonne
French Caesar • Aïoli Frites • Catalan Seafood Stew
Bone-In Veal Chop Paillard • Mousse au Chocolat

SCAN FOR MENU

SOME BASICS

Reservations:	YES
Spirits:	BEER/WINE
Parking:	STREET
Outdoor Dining:	NO

CHAZ 51 STEAKHOUSE

549 US-41(Bypass North)
941-484-6200
chaz51steakhouse.com

VENICE	STEAKHOUSE	COST: $$$

HOURS: Sun-Thur, 4PM to 9PM • Fri & Sat, 4PM to 9:30PM
Happy Hour Daily

WHAT TO EXPECT: Prime Angus Beef • Wine Tastings
Private Dining Available • Craft Cocktails

BEST BITES: Blue Crab Martini • Mussels Parisienne
Iceberg Wedge BLT • USDA Prime NY Strip Steak
Panko Crusted Gulf Grouper • Sautéed Spinach With Garlic

SCAN FOR MENU

SOME BASICS

Reservations:	YES
Spirits:	FULL BAR
Parking:	LOT
Outdoor Dining:	NO

CIRCO
1435 2nd Street
941-253-0978
circosrq.com

DOWNTOWN	MEXICAN	COST: $$

HOURS: Mon, 4PM to 10PM • Tue, 11AM to 9PM • Sun, 12PM to 9PM
Wed-Thur, 9PM to 10PM • Fri & Sat, 12PM to 10PM

WHAT TO EXPECT: Super Casual • "Taco & Bourbon Joint"
Good For A Group • Catering Available

BEST BITES: Chips & Elote Corn Salsa • Tijuana Salad
Tamale Cake • Picnic Chicken Tacos • Walking Taco
Mongolian Beef Taco • Ahi Poke Taco

SOME BASICS
SCAN FOR MENU

Reservations:	NO
Spirits:	FULL BAR
Parking:	STREET/GARAGE
Outdoor Dining:	YES

CLASICO ITALIAN CHOPHOUSE
1341 Main Street
941-203-5115
clasicosrq.com

DOWNTOWN	ITALIAN	COST: $$$

HOURS: Sun-Tues, 11AM to 11PM • Wed-Fri, 11AM to 12AM
Sat, 10AM to 12AM

WHAT TO EXPECT: Happy Hour • Private Event Space
Fun For A Date Night • Bustling on Weekends

BEST BITES: Crostinis • Pasta Dishes • Raw Bar
Fire Roasted Artichokes • Beef Carpaccio • Braised Short Rib
Pizzas! • Italian Chopped Salad

SOME BASICS
SCAN FOR MENU

Reservations:	YES
Spirits:	FULL BAR
Parking:	STREET/GARAGE
Outdoor Dining:	YES

THE COLUMBIA RESTAURANT
411 St. Armands Circle
941-388-3987
columbiarestaurant.com

ST. ARMANDS	CUBAN/SPANISH	COST: $$$

HOURS: Sun-Thur, 11AM to 9PM
Fri & Sat, 11AM to 10PM

WHAT TO EXPECT: Fantastic Sangria • Excellent Service
OpenTable Reservations • Very Busy In Season

BEST BITES: 1905 Salad • Cuban Black Bean Soup • Cuban Sandwich
Empanadas de Picadillo • La Completa Cubana
Snapper a la Rusa • Flan

SCAN FOR MENU

SOME BASICS
Reservations:	YES
Spirits:	FULL BAR
Parking:	STREET/GARAGE
Outdoor Dining:	YES

COMIDA
`NEW`

1534 State Street
941-324-5985
comidasrq.com

DOWNTOWN	LATIN	COST: $$

HOURS: Sun-Thur, 4PM to 10PM • Fri & Sat, 4PM to 11PM
Brunch - Sat & Sun, 10AM to 3PM

WHAT TO EXPECT: Tiny, Cute Place • Casual Latin Dining
Happy Hour Daily • Gluten Free

BEST BITES: Chilaquiles Verde & Rojo • Cobia Ceviche
Chili and Lime Tuna Crudo • Milanesa Fried Chicken
Wild Columbia River King Salmon • Columbia Flan Cafe Hola

SCAN FOR MENU

SOME BASICS
Reservations:	YES
Spirits:	FULL BAR
Parking:	STREET/GARAGE
Outdoor Dining:	YES

CONNORS STEAKHOUSE

3501 South Tamiami Trail
941-260-3232
connorsrestaurant.com

SOUTHGATE	STEAKHOUSE	COST: $$$

HOURS: Sun-Thur, 11AM to 10PM
Fri & Sat, 11AM to 11PM

WHAT TO EXPECT: Lots Of Parking • Large Menu
Lots Of Wines By The Glass • OpenTable Reservations

BEST BITES: Jumbo Shrimp Cocktail • Truffled Deviled Eggs
Lobster Crab Bisque • Espresso Rub Ribeye
Chilean Sea Bass Oscar • Chicken Piccata

SOME BASICS

SCAN FOR MENU

Reservations:	YES
Spirits:	FULL BAR
Parking:	LOT/VALET
Outdoor Dining:	YES

CORKSCREW DELI

4982 South Tamiami Trail
941-925-3955
corkscrewdeli.com

THE LANDINGS	DELI	COST: $$

HOURS: Mon-Sat, 10AM to 4PM
CLOSED SUNDAY

WHAT TO EXPECT: Deli Menu • Lots Of Parking • Since 1994!
Great For A Quick Lunch • Daily Specials

BEST BITES: Italian Sub Sandwich • The El Paso Sandwich
Hot Paisano Sandwich • Vermont Wrap • BLT
Sandwich + Soup Or Salad Combos!

SOME BASICS

SCAN FOR MENU

Reservations:	NO
Spirits:	NONE
Parking:	LOT
Outdoor Dining:	YES

THE COTTAGE
153 Avenida Messina
941-312-9300
cottagesiestakey.com

SIESTA KEY	AMERICAN	COST: $$

HOURS: Sun-Thur, 11AM to 10PM
Fri & Sat, 11AM to 11PM

WHAT TO EXPECT: Tapas • Fantastic Service • Great Outdoor Dining
Vacation Atmosphere • Nice Craft Beer Selection

BEST BITES: Blackened Tuna Club • Billionaire Burger!!
Lobster Bisque • Tuna Tacoshimi • Black Mussels
Beef Short Ribs • Patio Salad

SCAN FOR MENU

SOME BASICS
Reservations:	NO
Spirits:	FULL BAR
Parking:	STREET/VALET
Outdoor Dining:	YES

CRAB & FIN
420 St. Armands Circle
941-388-3964
crabfinrestaurant.com

ST. ARMANDS	SEAFOOD	COST: $$$

HOURS: Sun-Thur, 11:30AM to 9PM
Fri & Sat, 11:30AM to 9:30PM

WHAT TO EXPECT: Fresh Seafood Daily • Sunday Brunch
Online Reservations • Early Dining Options

BEST BITES: Norwegian Sea Opilio Snow Crab • Raw Bar
Whole Local Mangrove Snapper • Alaskan Halibut
Gazpacho • Prime Butcher's Block Pork Ribeye

SCAN FOR MENU

SOME BASICS
Reservations:	YES
Spirits:	FULL BAR
Parking:	STREET/LOT
Outdoor Dining:	YES

CUBA 1958

1766 Main Street
941-280-1958
cuba1958.com

DOWNTOWN	CUBAN	COST: $$$

HOURS: Lunch: Mon-Sat, 11:30AM to 3PM
Dinner: Mon-Sat: 4PM to 10PM • CLOSED SUNDAY

WHAT TO EXPECT: Authentic Cuban Cuisine • Friendly Staff
Great For A Date • Happy Hour Specials (Mon-Fri)

BEST BITES: Ropa Vieja • Ensalada Tropical • Cuban Special 1958
Empanadas de Pollo • Churrasco • Vaca Frita
Arroz con Pollo • Flan • Tres Leches

SOME BASICS

SCAN FOR MENU

Reservations:	YES
Spirits:	FULL BAR
Parking:	LOT
Outdoor Dining:	YES

THE DAIQUIRI DECK

5250 Ocean Boulevard*
941-349-8697
daiquirideficsiestakey.com

SIESTA KEY	AMERICAN	COST: $$

HOURS: Lunch & Dinner Daily

WHAT TO EXPECT: Island Atmosphere • The WALL of Daiquiris!
Raw Bar Next Door • Perfect Stop After the Beach

BEST BITES: Florida Gator Bites • Deck'd Out Fries
Mojo Cuban Sandwich • Crab Cake BLT • Jambalaya
Chopped Cobb Salad • Key Lime Pie

SOME BASICS

SCAN FOR MENU

Reservations:	NO
Spirits:	FULL BAR
Parking:	STREET
Outdoor Dining:	YES

DARRELL'S

215 South Tamiami Trail
941-485-9900
darrellsrestaurant.net

VENICE	BBQ	COST: $$

HOURS: Daily, 11AM to 9PM

WHAT TO EXPECT: BBQ! • Super Casual Atmosphere
Private Dining Room Available • Great For Families

BEST BITES: Fried Okra • Pork Nachos • Darrell's Famous Wings
Louisiana Gumbo • Piggyback Burger • Brisket Sandwich
St. Louis Ribs • Hungry Heifer • Banana Pudding!

SCAN FOR MENU

SOME BASICS

Reservations:	NO
Spirits:	BEER/WINE
Parking:	LOT
Outdoor Dining:	NO

DARUMA JAPANESE STEAK HOUSE

5459 Fruitville Road*
941-342-6600
darumarestaurant.com

SARASOTA CROSSINGS	ASIAN	COST: $$

HOURS: Daily, 5PM to 10PM

WHAT TO EXPECT: Fun Date Night • Good For Kids
Private Parties • Fun Place For A Group Dinner

BEST BITES: Gyoza • Negamaki • DaRuMa Teppan Combinations
Sushi • Shrimp Tempura • YoYo Shrimp
Warm & Cold Sake Choices

SCAN FOR MENU

SOME BASICS

Reservations:	YES
Spirits:	FULL BAR
Parking:	LOT
Outdoor Dining:	NO

D'CORATO RISTORANTE
322 South Washington Boulevard
941-330-1300
dcoratoristorante.com

DOWNTOWN	ITALIAN	COST: $$$

HOURS: Tue-Sat, 5:30PM to 9:30PM

WHAT TO EXPECT: Monthly Specials • Casual Atmosphere
Classic Italian Cuisine • Online Reservations

BEST BITES: Mussels alla Birra • Caprese Salad • Enzo Salad
Lasagna Bolognese • Melanzane Parmigiana
Saltimbocca • Risotto ai Funghi

SCAN FOR MENU

SOME BASICS
Reservations:	YES
Spirits:	BEER/WINE
Parking:	LOT
Outdoor Dining:	NO

DEEP LAGOON SEAFOOD & OYSTER HOUSE
482 Blackburn Point Road
941-770-3337
deeplagoon.com

OSPREY	AMERICAN	COST: $$$

HOURS: Daily, 11AM to 10PM

WHAT TO EXPECT: FL Outdoor Dining • Great Water Views
11-4 "Light Lunch" Menu

BEST BITES: Oysters Rockefeller • Scallop Ceviche
Big Chill Seafood Tower • Lobster Bisque • Stuffed Hogfish
Seared Ahi Tuna Salad • Raw Bar • Bone-In Ribeye

SCAN FOR MENU

SOME BASICS
Reservations:	YES
Spirits:	FULL BAR
Parking:	LOT
Outdoor Dining:	YES

DER DUTCHMAN

3713 Bahia Vista Street
941-955-8007
dhgroup.com

PINECRAFT	AMISH	COST: $$

HOURS: Mon-Sat, 7AM to 8PM
CLOSED SUNDAY

WHAT TO EXPECT: Good For Kids • Best Buffet In The U.S.
Home Cooking • Great Pie • Groups Welcome

BEST BITES: Roast Beef, Turkey, Or Meatloaf Manhattan
Homemade Soups • Broasted Chicken • Pie!
Breakfast, Lunch & Dinner Buffet

SCAN FOR MENU

SOME BASICS

Reservations:	NO
Spirits:	NONE
Parking:	LOT
Outdoor Dining:	NO

DIM SUM KING

8194 Tourist Center Drive
941-306-5848
dimsumsarasota.com

LAKEWOOD RANCH	ASIAN	COST: $$

HOURS: Lunch, Wed-Mon, 11AM to 2:30PM
Dinner, Wed-Mon, 5PM to 8:30PM • CLOSED TUESDAY

WHAT TO EXPECT: Dim Sum!! • Very Casual Atmosphere
Great For A Quick Lunch • Lots Of Parking Available

BEST BITES: Steamed Spare Ribs In Black Bean Sauce
Chicken ShuMai • Shanghai Style Dumplings
Honey Glazed BBQ Pork • Crispy Shrimp Toast

SCAN FOR MENU

SOME BASICS

Reservations:	NO
Spirits:	BEER/WINE
Parking:	LOT
Outdoor Dining:	NO

DIVAN

6525 Superior Avenue
941-924-3030
divanturkishcuisine.com

GULF GATE	TURKISH	COST: $$

HOURS: Mon, 4PM to 9PM • Breakfast: Tue-Sun, 10AM to 2PM
Lunch & Dinner: Tue-Sun from 2PM

WHAT TO EXPECT: Delicious Turkish Cuisine • Family Owned
Casual Atmosphere • A Fun Group Dinner!

BEST BITES: Sucuk & Cheese Panini • Doner Pita/Wrap
Babaganoush • Stuffed Grape Leaves • Shepherd Salad
Iskender • Lamb Chops • Walnut Baklava

SOME BASICS

		SCAN FOR MENU
Reservations:	YES	
Spirits:	BEER/WINE	
Parking:	LOT	
Outdoor Dining:	NO	

SARASOTA WEEKEND BRUNCHES

Arts & Central • 611 Central Ave. • 306-2356
WHAT TO EXPECT: Special Sunday brunch menu. Build Your Own Benedict! Enjoy a Guava Mimosa with your meal.

Kolukan • 6644 Gateway Ave. • 921-3133
WHAT TO EXPECT: Brunch Mexican style! Upscale, but still casual. Don't pass on the Tres Leches French Toast.

Rosemary & Thyme • 511 N. Orange Ave. • 955-7600
WHAT TO EXPECT: Special Sunday brunch menu. Classic brunch dishes plus new twists on old favs. The Seafood Quiche!

Summer House • 149 Avenida Messina • 260-2675
WHAT TO EXPECT: One of the best brunches in SRQ. All you can eat. Makes any Sunday feel special. Save room for dessert!

DOUBLE DEEZ CHICAGO STYLE HOT DOGS

3009 Gulf Drive N.
941-251-5595
doubledeezami.com

HOLMES BEACH	AMERICAN	COST: $

HOURS: Wed-Sat, 12PM to 8PM • Sun, 12PM to 7PM
CLOSED MONDAY & TUESDAY

WHAT TO EXPECT: It's A "Chicago" Hot Dog Stand! • Family Friendly
Super Casual • Great For A Quick Lunch On The Go

BEST BITES: Chicago Style Hot Dog • Italian Beef Sandwich
Maxwell Street Polish Sausage • Double Deez Wrigley Combo
Cheesy Beef

SCAN FOR INFO

SOME BASICS
Reservations:	NO
Spirits:	NONE
Parking:	LOT
Outdoor Dining:	YES

DOUGHBOY SWIFT   NEW

2881 Clark Road
941-315-7011
doughboyswift.com

MERCHANT'S POINTE	ITALIAN	COST: $$

HOURS: Daily, 3PM to Close

WHAT TO EXPECT: Small, Relaxed Pizza Place • Good For Families
Sports On TV • Great Meet Up Place • Two Slice Specials

BEST BITES: Pizza, Pizza! • Meatballs & Ricotta • Wings & "Nuggs"
Smash Burger • Meatball Smash • Chopped Italian Salad
Cheesecake • Craft Beers on Tap

SCAN FOR MENU

SOME BASICS
Reservations:	NO
Spirits:	BEER/WINE
Parking:	LOT
Outdoor Dining:	NO

DRIFT KITCHEN
700 Benjamin Franklin Drive (Lido Beach Resort)
941-388-2161
lidobeachresort.com/dining/drift

LIDO KEY	AMERICAN	COST: $$

HOURS: Daily, 7AM to 10PM
Happy Hour Daily, 4PM to 6PM

WHAT TO EXPECT: Upscale Dining • 180° Gulf Views
Lido Beach Resort

BEST BITES: Traditional Eggs Benedict • Cuban Eggs
Crispy Crab Cake • Charcuterie Board • Lido Caesar
Pizza & Flatbreads • Rigatoni Bolognese • Key Lime Pie

SOME BASICS

SCAN FOR MENU

Reservations:	YES
Spirits:	FULL BAR
Parking:	LOT
Outdoor Dining:	NO

DRUNKEN POET CAFÉ
1572 Main Street
941-955-8404
drunkenpoetcafesrq.com

DOWNTOWN	THAI	COST: $$

HOURS: Sun-Thur, 11AM to 10PM
Fri & Sat, 11AM to 12AM

WHAT TO EXPECT: Casual Atmosphere • Good Vegan Options
Later Night Dining • Great For Small Groups

BEST BITES: Pinky In The Blanket • Crispy Duck Basil
Pad Thai • Pad Kee Mao • Thai Spare Ribs
Duck Noodle Soup • Sushi!! • Fried Ice Cream

SOME BASICS

SCAN FOR MENU

Reservations:	YES
Spirits:	BEER/WINE
Parking:	STREET
Outdoor Dining:	YES

DRY DOCK WATERFRONT RESTAURANT

412 Gulf of Mexico Drive (Marker 6 By Boat)
941-383-0102
drydockwaterfrontgrill.com

LONGBOAT KEY	SEAFOOD	COST: $$

HOURS: Sun-Thur, 11AM to 9PM
Fri & Sat, 11AM to 10PM

WHAT TO EXPECT: Great Water View • Local Seafood • Happy Hour
Good For Groups • OpenTable Reservations

BEST BITES: Lobster Bites • Oysters Rockefeller • Fishcamp Chowder
Caesar Salad • Linguine With Clams • Boathouse Tacos
Citrus Grouper • Ribeye Steak • Lobster Rolls

SCAN FOR MENU

SOME BASICS

Reservations:	YES
Spirits:	FULL BAR
Parking:	LOT
Outdoor Dining:	YES

THE DUO - DÖNER & DELI

5049 Ocean Boulevard
941-298-9660

SIESTA KEY	TURKISH	COST: $$

HOURS: Daily, Noon to Close

WHAT TO EXPECT: Turkish To-Go! • Super Casual • Parking!!
Family Owned/Chef Driven • Great For A Beach Day

BEST BITES: Döner Sandwich, Wrap Or Plate • Pizza Toast
Grilled Kielbasa • Duo Smash Burger!
Waffle Roll • Slushies! • Espresso

SCAN FOR MENU

SOME BASICS

Reservations:	NO
Spirits:	NONE
Parking:	LOT
Outdoor Dining:	NO

DUTCH VALLEY RESTAURANT

6721 South Tamiami Trail
941-924-1770
dutchvalleyrestaurant.net

SOUTH TRAIL	AMERICAN	COST: $$

HOURS: Daily, 7AM to 9PM

WHAT TO EXPECT: Old School Diner Feel • Lots Of Parking
Open 365 Days A Year! • Great For A Carry Out

BEST BITES: Broasted Chicken • Daily Specials • BLT Sandwich
Eggs Benedict Florentine • Homemade Soups
Open Faced Turkey Sandwich • Burgers

SCAN FOR MENU

SOME BASICS

Reservations:	NO
Spirits:	BEER/WINE
Parking:	LOT
Outdoor Dining:	NO

DUVAL'S FRESH. LOCAL. SEAFOOD.

1435 Main Street
941-312-4001
duvalsfreshlocalseafood.com

DOWNTOWN	AMERICAN	COST: $$$

HOURS: Sun-Thur, 11AM to 10PM
Fri & Sat, 11AM to 11PM

WHAT TO EXPECT: Brunch • OpenTable Reservations
Great Happy Hour • Free Shuttle To The Restaurant

BEST BITES: Lump Crab Cake • Seafood Bruschetta • Po' Boys!
Duval's BLT • Chicken Cutlet Parmesan • Wedge Salad
Bouillabaisse • Duval's Seafood Sampler • Bread Pudding

SCAN FOR MENU

SOME BASICS

Reservations:	YES
Spirits:	FULL BAR
Parking:	STREET
Outdoor Dining:	YES

1818 GRILL
1818 South Osprey Avenue
941-955-1818
the1818grill.com

SOUTHSIDE VILLAGE	AMERICAN	COST: $$

HOURS: Mon-Fri, 11AM to 9PM • Sat, 4PM to 9PM
CLOSED SUNDAY

WHAT TO EXPECT: Casual • Reservations • Great Lunch Meet Up
"Gulf Coast" Cuisine

BEST BITES: Blackened Calamari • Greek Hummus Plate
Buffalo Chicken Cobb Salad • The Ultimate Wedge
German Pork Smash Burger • Chicken Pot Pie

SCAN FOR MENU

SOME BASICS
Reservations:	YES
Spirits:	BEER/WINE
Parking:	STREET
Outdoor Dining:	YES

---

83 TAVERN
8383 South Tamiami Trail
941-203-5312
83tavern.com

NEW

SOUTH TRAIL	AMERICAN	COST: $$

HOURS: Sun-Thur, 11AM to 9PM
Fri & Sat, 11AM to 10PM

WHAT TO EXPECT: Tavern Fare • Super Casual • COLD Drinks
Midwest "Tavern Cut" Pizza • 15 TVs For Sports Watching

BEST BITES: Pizza • Buffalo Wontons • BBQ Chicken Salad
Wings • Americana Burger • Crispy Fish Tacos
Burgundy Braised Beef • Coca Cola Pork Ribs

SCAN FOR MENU

SOME BASICS
Reservations:	NO
Spirits:	FULL BAR
Parking:	LOT
Outdoor Dining:	YES

EL TORO BRAVO
3218 Clark Road
941-924-0006
eltorobravosarasota.com

MEXICAN	COST: $$

HOURS: Tue-Thur, 11:30AM to 9PM • Fri, 11:30AM to 10PM
Sat, 12PM to 10PM • Sun, 12PM to 9PM • Mon, 3PM to 9PM

WHAT TO EXPECT: Great For Families • Super Casual Dining
Usually Busy • Online Reservations • Lots Of Parking

BEST BITES: Jalapeños Rellenos • Queso Blanco
Shrimp Chimichanga • Combination Plates
Chips & Homemade Salsa • Deep Fried Cheesecake

SCAN FOR MENU

SOME BASICS
Reservations:	YES
Spirits:	BEER/WINE
Parking:	LOT
Outdoor Dining:	NO

ELEMENT
1413 Main Street
941-724-8585
elementsrq.com

DOWNTOWN	AMERICAN	COST: $$$

HOURS: Lunch: Tues-Fri, 11AM to 2PM • CLOSED MONDAY
Dinner: Tues-Sun, 4PM • Sunday Brunch, 10:30AM to 2PM

WHAT TO EXPECT: Five Points Location • Happy Hour Daily
Adult Bar Scene • Oyster Specials "2 Buck A Shuck"

BEST BITES: Flaming Saganaki • Steak Tartare • Shrimp Cocktail
Beet Salad • Oysters Rockefeller • Creekstone Prime Burger
Roasted Chateaubriand • Apple Cobbler a la Mode

SCAN FOR MENU

SOME BASICS
Reservations:	YES
Spirits:	FULL BAR
Parking:	STREET/VALET
Outdoor Dining:	YES

ENRICH BISTRO
5239 Manatee Avenue W.
941-289-1299
enrichbistro.com

BRADENTON	GLOBAL CUISINE	COST: $$$

HOURS: Lunch: Mon-Sat, 11AM to 2:30PM • CLOSED SUNDAY
Dinner: Mon-Thur, 5PM to 11PM • Fri & Sat Until 1AM

WHAT TO EXPECT: Great For A Date • "Global" Flavors
Finer Dining Experience • Nice Beer Selection

BEST BITES: THE Calamari Salad • Caviar En Pave • Skirt Steak
Nacho Of The Week • Dry Aged USDA Prime Strip
Yellowfin Tuna • Maple Leaf Farms "Duck Duo"

SCAN FOR MENU

SOME BASICS
Reservations:	YES
Spirits:	FULL BAR
Parking:	LOT
Outdoor Dining:	NO

EUPHEMIA HAYE
5540 Gulf of Mexico Drive
941-383-3633
euphemiahaye.com

LONGBOAT KEY	AMERICAN	COST: $$$$

HOURS: Tue-Thur, 5:30PM to 9PM • Fri & Sat, 5PM to 9:30PM
Sun, 5:30PM to 9PM • CLOSED MONDAY

WHAT TO EXPECT: Great For A Date • The Haye Loft For Dessert!
Fine Dining Experience • Great For Special Occasions

BEST BITES: Snails Leslie • Classic Caesar Salad
Tagliatelle Alla Carbonara • Roasted Duckling
Euphemia's Prime Peppered Steak • Key West Snapper

SCAN FOR MENU

SOME BASICS
Reservations:	YES
Spirits:	FULL BAR
Parking:	LOT
Outdoor Dining:	NO

15 SOUTH BY NAPULE

15 South Boulevard of the Presidents
941-867-8081
15south.net

ST ARMANDS	ITALIAN	COST: $$$

HOURS: Sun-Thur, 11AM to 9PM
Fri & Sat, 11AM to 10PM

WHAT TO EXPECT: Casual Classic Italian Fare • Fantastic Pizza!
St. Armands Location • Busy During Season

BEST BITES: Cotto Panini • Tricolore Panuozzi • Charcuterie
THE PIZZA!! • Ricco Salad • Spaghetti Alle Vongole
Brodetto Di Mare • Tiramisu

SOME BASICS

SCAN FOR MENU

Reservations:	YES
Spirits:	FULL BAR
Parking:	STREET/GARAGE
Outdoor Dining:	YES

1592 WOOD FIRED KITCHEN & COCKTAILS

1592 Main Street
941-365-2234
1592srq.com

DOWNTOWN	GREEK	COST: $$

HOURS: Mon-Thur, 11AM to 10PM • Fri & Sat, 11AM to 11PM
Sun, 4PM to 10PM

WHAT TO EXPECT: Great Casual Dining • Great Happy Hour
Nice Street-Side Dining • Good Downtown Lunch Spot

BEST BITES: Farmers Market Hummus • Saganaki
Spicy Feta Spread • Pulled Lamb Open Faced Pita
Moussaka • Montreal's "Poutine" • Pizza!

SOME BASICS

SCAN FOR MENU

Reservations:	YES
Spirits:	BEER/WINE
Parking:	STREET
Outdoor Dining:	YES

Aunt Joyce's Macaroni Salad

Pork Roll Pete's
Joyce Pizzichillo

INGREDIENTS

1 lb elbow macaroni
1 cup Hellmann's Mayonnaise
2 cans albacore tuna fish
1 cup celery, diced
¼ cup onion, diced
Salt and Pepper to taste

METHOD

Fill a large pot with water (about 4-6 quarts for 1 pound pasta). Bring it to a rolling boil over high heat. Add the elbow macaroni and stir right away so the pasta does not stick together or at the bottom.

Cook the macaroni for 6-7 minutes until al dente. It should be tender but still slightly firm in the center. Drain quickly and pour into a colander.

While the elbow macaroni is cooling, wash your hands and wear gloves to break apart the tuna fish very finely into a large bowl, no chunks!

Wash celery stalks. Cut the stalks into 3 strips and cut into small pieces. Add the cooled elbow macaroni, fine tuna fish, and diced celery into the large bowl. Add 1 cup of mayonnaise, salt and pepper to taste and stir until everything is evenly coated!

Serve it cold and enjoy Aunt Joyce's Macaroni Salad!

Pork Roll Pete's is a family owned establishment featuring the best NJ has to offer. PRP introduces the finest bagels, sandwiches, and foods in the Bradenton area. From our New York Watermaker, fresh baked bagels, Jersey Pork Roll and Italian imports, we have all ingredients!

Aunt Joyce resides in Hazlet, NJ with her husband, Billy. Aunt Joyce's Macaroni Salad is fresh, flavorful, and packed with love!

We've Got Your Sarasota Restaurant News!

sarasota bites

SUBSCRIBE TODAY

THE FAT RABBIT
1359 Main Street
941-780-115
fatrabbitpub.com

DOWNTOWN	AMERICAN	COST: $$

HOURS: Tue-Sun, Lunch & Dinner
CLOSED MONDAY

WHAT TO EXPECT: Hidden On The 2nd Floor! • "Neighborhood Pub"
Good Burgers & Wings • Catering Available

BEST BITES: Black and Blue Chicken • Pretzel Flight
A "Loaded" Tots Menu! • Grown Up Grilled Cheese
Bayside Burger • Sriracha Dry Rub Wings

SCAN FOR MENU

SOME BASICS
Reservations:	NO
Spirits:	FULL BAR
Parking:	STREET
Outdoor Dining:	NO

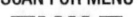

FIGARO BISTRO
1944 Hillview Street
941-960-2109
figaro-bistro.com

SOUTHSIDE VILLAGE	FRENCH	COST: $$$

HOURS: Tue-Thur, 5PM to 9PM
Fri & Sat, 5PM to 9:30PM CLOSED SUNDAY & MONDAY

WHAT TO EXPECT: Authentic, Upscale French Cuisine
Nice Wine List • Try The Escargots De Bourgogne

BEST BITES: Escargots Tradition • Salade Lyonnaise
Moules Frites • Boeuf Bourguignon • Filet de Bœuf
Magret de Canard Aux Myrtiles • Crêpe Suzette

SCAN FOR MENU

SOME BASICS
Reservations:	YES
Spirits:	BEER/WINE
Parking:	STREET
Outdoor Dining:	YES

FINS AT SHARKY'S
1600 Harbor Drive South
941-999-3467
finsatsharkys.com

VENICE	AMERICAN	COST: $$$

HOURS: Lunch, Daily, 11:45PM to 2:30PM
Dinner, Daily, 4PM to 10PM

WHAT TO EXPECT: Beachfront Dining • "Fins Frenzy" Happy Hour
Good Wine List • "Steakhouse With A Serious Seafood Side"

BEST BITES: Cheese & Charcuterie Plate • Josper Grilled Octopus
Lobster Potato Nachos • Heirloom Tomato Caprese
Smoked Rib Eye • Faroe Island Salmon

SCAN FOR MENU

SOME BASICS
Reservations:	YES
Spirits:	FULL BAR
Parking:	LOT
Outdoor Dining:	YES

FLAVIO'S ON SIESTA
5239 Ocean Boulevard
941-349-0995
flaviosbrickovenandbar.com

SIESTA KEY	ITALIAN	COST: $$$

HOURS: Daily, 4PM to 10PM
Happy Hour, 4PM to 6PM

WHAT TO EXPECT: Homemade Italian Cuisine • Brick Oven Pizza
Good "Adult" Bar Scene • Siesta Village Location

BEST BITES: Brick Oven Pizza! • Mozzarella in Carrozza
Spiedino Di Gamberi • Burrata e Prosciutto
Insalata Cesare • Pappardelle Ai Porcini • Nodino Di Vitello

SOME BASICS
SCAN FOR MENU

Reservations:	YES
Spirits:	FULL BAR
Parking:	LOT
Outdoor Dining:	YES

FLORENCE AND THE SPICE BOYS
4990 South Tamiami Trail
941-405-3890
florenceandthespiceboys.com

THE LANDINGS	MIDDLE EASTERN	COST: $$

HOURS: Mon-Sat, 11AM to 8PM
CLOSED SUNDAY

WHAT TO EXPECT: Israeli-Influenced Cuisine • Vegan/Veg Options
Nice Outdoor Dining Space • Convenient Online Ordering

BEST BITES: Chicken Shawarma Salad! • Hummus Sweet Corn
Harissa Shrimp Skewer • Corn Ribs • Bhel Puri
Mushroom Pita • Spice Boys Organic Date "Snickers"

SOME BASICS
SCAN FOR MENU

Reservations:	NO
Spirits:	NONE
Parking:	LOT
Outdoor Dining:	YES

FLOWER CHILD

6532 University Parkway
941-373-0199
iamaflowerchild.com/locations/flower-child-sarasota-fl

UTC	AMERICAN	COST: $$

HOURS: Daily, 11AM to 9PM

WHAT TO EXPECT: Healthier Food Options • Vegan, Veg, Gluten Free
Upscale Fast Casual • Great For A Quick Healthy Lunch

BEST BITES: Korean BBQ Beef "Bulgogi"• Chicken Yakisoba Noodles
Chicken Enchiladas • Black Bean Falafel Wrap
Chocolate Chip Cashew Cookie • Chocolate Pudding

SCAN FOR MENU

SOME BASICS

Reservations:	NO
Spirits:	BEER/WINE
Parking:	LOT
Outdoor Dining:	NO

FOCACCIA SANDWICH + BAKERY

2300 Bee Ridge Road
941-924-226
focacciasandwich.com

THE COLONNADE	DELI	COST: $$

HOURS: Tues-Sat, 11AM to 3PM
CLOSED SUNDAY & MONDAY

WHAT TO EXPECT: Fresh Baked Bread • Great For A To Go
Limited Seating • Plenty Of Parking

BEST BITES: Porchetta Sandwich • Italian Sandwich
Prime Rib Sandwich • Charred Artichokes
Roasted Tomato Bisque • Daily Sandwich Specials

SCAN FOR MENU

SOME BASICS

Reservations:	NO
Spirits:	NONE
Parking:	LOT
Outdoor Dining:	YES

FOOD + BEER
6528 Superior Avenue*
941-952-3361
eatfooddrinkbeer.com

GULF GATE	AMERICAN	COST: $$

HOURS: Mon-Thur, 11AM to 1AM • Fri, 11AM to 2AM
Sat, 10AM to 2AM • Sun, 10AM to 1AM

WHAT TO EXPECT: Super Casual • Good Local Beer Selection
Later Night Menu • Sat & Sun Brunch

BEST BITES: Down The Hatch Burger • Malibu Barbie Wrap
Birria Tacos • Cali Hot Cobb Bowl • Fried Goat Cheese
Buffalo Chicken Wedge • Red Velvet Oreos

SCAN FOR MENU

SOME BASICS
Reservations:	NO
Spirits:	BEER/WINE
Parking:	STREET/LOT
Outdoor Dining:	NO

FORK & HEN
1990 Main Street
941-444-7094
forkandhenssrq.com

NORTH TRAIL	AMERICAN	COST: $$

HOURS: Tues-Thur, 11:30AM to 7:30PM • Fri-Sun, 11:30AM to 8PM
CLOSED MONDAY

WHAT TO EXPECT: Chef-Driven Menu • Super Casual Dining
Scratch Kitchen • New Downtown Location (2025)

BEST BITES: Fork & Hen Cobb Salad • "OG" Chicken Sandwich
Low Country Shrimp & Grits • Stepbrother Burger
Best Damn Mac N Cheese • Fried Chicken & Waffles

SCAN FOR MENU

SOME BASICS
Reservations:	NO
Spirits:	NONE
Parking:	LOT
Outdoor Dining:	YES

FRESTA'S ITALIAN AMERICAN CUISINE `NEW`

6392 Lockwood Ridge Road
941-203-8467
frestasitalian.com

PARKWAY COLLECTION	ITALIAN	COST: $$$

HOURS: Tue-Thur, 11AM to 9PM • Fri & Sat, 11AM to 10PM
Sun, 11AM to 9PM • CLOSED MONDAY

WHAT TO EXPECT: Upscale Casual • Limited Bar Area Seating
Craft Cocktails • Nice Outdoor Dining Space

BEST BITES: Pizza! • Garlic Knots • Meatballs & Whipped Ricotta
Roasted Beets & Burrata Salad • Chicken Cutlet
Original Philly Cheese Steak • Shrimp Gamberetti

SCAN FOR MENU

SOME BASICS

Reservations:	YES
Spirits:	FULL BAR
Parking:	LOT
Outdoor Dining:	YES

FUEGO COMIDA & TEQUILA

11615 FL-70
941-751-5252
fuegotequilalounge.com

LWR	MEXICAN	COST: $$

HOURS: Daily, 4PM to Close
Brunch: Fri-Sun, 11AM to 4PM

WHAT TO EXPECT: Craft Tequila Lounge • Coastal Mexican Cuisine
Upscale Atmosphere • Happy Hour

BEST BITES: Salsa Trip • Fuego Crab Cake • Birria Empanadas
Ceviche • Beet & Watermelon Salad • Fuego Oscar
Short Rib • Mexico City Garlic Noodles

SCAN FOR MENU

SOME BASICS

Reservations:	YES
Spirits:	FULL BAR
Parking:	LOT
Outdoor Dining:	YES

GECKO'S GRILL & PUB
6606 South Tamiami Trail*
941-248-2020
geckosgrill.com

SOUTH TRAIL	AMERICAN	COST: $$

HOURS: Daily, 11AM to 10PM

WHAT TO EXPECT: Great To Watch A Game • Yelp Waitlist
Good Burgers • "American Pub Food"

BEST BITES: Blue Cheese Chips • Loaded Potato Scoops
Wings! • Black Beans & Rice • The Ultimate Cobb
Flatbreads • Wraps • Burgers • Cuban Sub

SOME BASICS
SCAN FOR MENU

Reservations:	NO
Spirits:	FULL BAR
Parking:	LOT
Outdoor Dining:	YES

THE GRASSHOPPER
7253 South Tamiami Trail
941-923-3688
thegrasshoppertexmex.com

SOUTH TRAIL	MEXICAN	COST: $$

HOURS: Mon-Sat, 11AM to 10PM
Happy Hour, 3:30PM to 5:30PM

WHAT TO EXPECT: Easy On The Wallet • Happy Hour
Good Cocktail Selection • Good For Groups

BEST BITES: Huevos Rancheros • Signature Queso • Guacamole
Combination Plate • Taco Plate • Tamale Plate
Veggie Chili Rellenos • Menudo

SOME BASICS
SCAN FOR MENU

Reservations:	YES
Spirits:	FULL BAR
Parking:	LOT
Outdoor Dining:	NO

GRAZE STREET AMI

3218 E. Bay Drive
941-896-6320
grazestreetami.com

HOLMES BEACH	AMERICAN	COST: $

HOURS: Wed-Fri, 11AM to 6PM • Sat, 10AM to 6PM
Sun, 10AM to 3PM • CLOSED MONDAY & TUESDAY

WHAT TO EXPECT: Bakery & Gourmet Shop • Super Casual
Limited Sandwich Menu

BEST BITES: Caprese Sandwich • Green Goddess Sandwich
Beachy BLT • Tuna Salad • Cookies Every Day!

SCAN FOR MENU

SOME BASICS
Reservations:	NO
Spirits:	NONE
Parking:	STREET
Outdoor Dining:	NO

THE GREEN ORCHID

1534 Mound Street (Selby Gardens)
941-265-8194
bestfood.com/restaurant/the-green-orchid

SELBY GARDENS	FARM TO TABLE	COST: $$

HOURS: Daily, 11AM to 3PM
Weekend Brunch

WHAT TO EXPECT: "Green" Restaurant • Light, Bright Dining Room
The Freshest Local Ingredients • Requires Selby Admission

BEST BITES: Spicy Korean Lettuce Wraps • Hand-Cut Truffle Fries
The Selby Reuben • Jennifer's "Rooftop Garden" Salad
Phil's Rhode Island Lobster Rolls • Key Lime Tart

SCAN FOR MENU

SOME BASICS
Reservations:	YES
Spirits:	FULL BAR
Parking:	GARAGE
Outdoor Dining:	YES

GROVE

10670 Boardwalk Loop
941-893-4321
grovelwr.com

LAKEWOOD RANCH	AMERICAN	COST: $$$

HOURS: Mon-Thur, 11:30AM to 10PM • Fri, 11:30AM to 10:30PM
Sat, 10AM to 10:30PM • Sun, 10AM to 10PM

WHAT TO EXPECT: Happy Hour • Culinary Cocktails
Weekend Brunch 10AM to 3PM • Wine Dinners

BEST BITES: Mussels & Blue • Thai Cauliflower • Tuna Nachos
Flatbreads • NE Clam Chowder • Baby Wedge Salad
Jambalaya • Sushi • Grouper Oscar • Pork Osso Bucco

SCAN FOR MENU

SOME BASICS
Reservations: YES
Spirits: FULL BAR
Parking: LOT
Outdoor Dining: YES

HARRY'S CONTINENTAL KITCHENS

525 St. Judes Drive
941-383-0777
harryskitchen.com

LONGBOAT KEY	AMERICAN	COST: $$$

HOURS: Restaurant - Daily, 9AM to 9PM
Deli - 11AM to 7PM

WHAT TO EXPECT: Great For A Date • Monthly Wine Events
Upscale Florida Dining • Visit The "Corner Store"

BEST BITES: Shrimp-Cargot • Harry's Famous Crab Cakes
Fresh Chunky Gazpacho • Sautéed Veal Medallions
Roast Maple Leaf Half Duckling • Peanut Butter Pie

SCAN FOR MENU

SOME BASICS
Reservations: YES
Spirits: FULL BAR
Parking: LOT
Outdoor Dining: YES

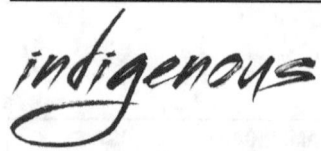

CORNMEAL CRUSTED PINE ISLAND
REDFISH WITH ALMOND ROMESCO

Indigenous
Chef Steve Phelps

INGREDIENTS
4 - 5 to 6 ounce redfish filets skinned, boned
salt
pepper
Bob's Red Mill fine cornmeal

ROMESCO
1 ¾ cup roasted red peppers
½ jalapeno chopped
3 cloves of garlic
½ tsp. smoked paprika
1 tbsp. basil fresh, chopped
1 tbsp. parsley fresh, chopped
2 cup toasted almonds (not too browned)
¼ cup tomato puree
1 tsp. tomato paste
¼ c sherry vinegar (more if you like)
¼ to ½ cup olive oil
salt to taste

METHOD - ROMESCO

Place all ingredients except oil, and sherry vinegar in Cuisinart
food processor. Puree all ingredients until beginning to smooth
(you don't want it real smooth).

With blade spinning slowly add vinegar and then slowly infuse oil.

Season and taste with salt.

METHOD - REDFISH

Pat dry fish with a paper towel. Season both sides with salt and pepper. Place cornmeal on a plate or bowl and press down the top side of the fish to coat.

Heat butter or oil in a skillet, saute cornmeal side in oil first at medium to low heat. Carefully flip fish and continue to cook through. Remove, serve and top with a generous amount of romesco.

Chef Steve Phelps opened Indigenous in 2011 to widespread acclaim, earning a James Beard Foundation semifinalist nomination for Best Chef: South. Staying true to its mission of conscientious sourcing, Indigenous features a seasonally changing menu that reflects the peak availability of ingredients and a steadfast commitment to sustainably harvested seafood, both wild-caught and responsibly farmed. The restaurant is in Sarasota's historic Towles Court at 239 S. Links Ave. For more info, call (941) 706.4740 or visit indigenoussarasota.com. For more info on Pine Island Redfish visit, pineislandredfish.com.

HIVE BAR
2881 Clark Road (Merchant's Pointe Plaza)
941-888-0382
hivebarsrq.com

MERCHANT'S POINTE	AMERICAN	COST: $$

HOURS: Most Days, 6PM

WHAT TO EXPECT: "Speakeasy" Type Restaurant • Special Events
Unique & Fun Dining Experience • Inside Dive Wine & Spirits

BEST BITES: The Big Mick Burger • Pasta Nights!
Empanada Menu! • Craft Cocktails • Nightly Set Food Menus

SOME BASICS
Reservations:	YES
Spirits:	FULL BAR
Parking:	LOT
Outdoor Dining:	NO

SCAN FOR INFO

THE HUB BAJA GRILL

5148 Ocean Boulevard
941-349-6800
thehubsiestakey.com

SIESTA KEY	AMERICAN	COST: $$

HOURS: Sun-Thur, 11AM to 10PM • Fri & Sat, 11AM to 11PM

WHAT TO EXPECT: Island Dining Experience • Good For Families
Busy In Season • Live Music Daily • Happy Hour Specials

BEST BITES: The Hub Margarita • Lobster Bisque • Baja Salad
Grande Nachos • Mahi Lettuce Wrap • The Hub Cuban
Short Rib Taco Sofrito • Baby Back Ribs

SCAN FOR MENU

SOME BASICS

Reservations:	NO
Spirits:	FULL BAR
Parking:	STREET
Outdoor Dining:	YES

ICHIBAN SUSHI

2724 Stickney Point Road
941-924-1611
sarasotaichiban.com

	JAPANESE	COST: $$

HOURS: Lunch: Mon-Fri, 11AM to 2PM
Dinner: Mon-Sat, 4PM to 9PM • CLOSED SUNDAY

WHAT TO EXPECT: All You Can Eat Sushi • Good For Families
Fun For Groups • Boba Tea Bar

BEST BITES: Krab Rangoon • Pan Fried Dumplings • Wonton Soup
Sushi • Sashimi • Hand Rolls • Lo-Mein
Udon Noodle Bowls • Bento Boxes • Sushi Specials

SCAN FOR MENU

SOME BASICS

Reservations:	NO
Spirits:	BEER/WINE
Parking:	LOT
Outdoor Dining:	NO

BURGER TIME!
SOME OF SARASOTA'S BEST

The Cottage • 153 Avenida Messina • 312-9300
WHAT TO EXPECT: Upscale casual on Siesta Key. The Billionaire Burger will not disappoint. Grab a cold craft beer to drink!

Hive Bar • 2881 Clark Rd. • 888-0382
WHAT TO EXPECT: Delicious "smash style" burgers. Usually on Thursdays. This is one of Sarasota's unique dining experiences.

Indigenous • 239 S. Links Ave. • 706-4740
WHAT TO EXPECT: This one is always a pleasant surprise. Chef Phelps puts out a delicious burger. Can you say, bacon jam?

Island House Tap & Grill • 5110 Ocean Blvd. • 487-8116
WHAT TO EXPECT: They have a super secret prep method that turns out a perfectly cooked, juicy, and delicious burger every time!

Lucky 8 • 1812 S. Osprey Ave. • 779-5299
WHAT TO EXPECT: NOLA focused cuisine. They also serve a fantastic smashburger. Single or a double. It's the "Lucky Sauce."

Mouthole Smashburgers • 2637 Mall Dr. • 746-4653
WHAT TO EXPECT: If you like a smash-style burger then this is your spot. Simple, delicious burgers. Locals love these!

Patrick's 1481 • 1481 Main St. • 955-1481
WHAT TO EXPECT: It's all about the burger at Patrick's. This restaurant is a downtown institution. Try it and you'll know why.

Shakespeare's • 3550 S. Osprey Ave. • 364-5938
WHAT TO EXPECT: A caramelized onion & Brie burger! English pub atmosphere. Lots and lots of craft beer to wash it all down.

Read Our Yearlong Burger Series
A BURGER A WEEK!

INDIGENOUS RESTAURANT
239 South Links Avenue
941-706-4740
indigenoussarasota.com

TOWLES COURT	AMERICAN	COST: $$$

HOURS: Tues-Sat, 5:30PM to 8:30PM
CLOSED SUNDAY & MONDAY

WHAT TO EXPECT: Great For A Date • Fine Dining, Casual Feel
Towles Court Neighborhood • Limited Outdoor Seating

BEST BITES: Wild Mushroom Bisque • Red Curry Fish Dip
Cobia Crudo • Pork Funchi • My Uncle's Burger
Everglades Baked Shrimp & Scallops • Buttermilk Pie

SCAN FOR MENU

SOME BASICS

Reservations:	YES
Spirits:	BEER/WINE
Parking:	LOT/STREET
Outdoor Dining:	YES

INKAWASI RESTAURANT
10667 Boardwalk Loop
941-360-1110
inkawasirestaurant.com

LAKEWOOD RANCH	PERUVIAN	COST: $$

HOURS: Mon-Thur, 12PM to 9PM • Fri & Sat, 12PM to 10PM
Sunday, 12PM to 8PM

WHAT TO EXPECT: Casual Peruvian • Lakewood Ranch Main Street
Lots Of Parking

BEST BITES: Chicharroncitos de Puerco • Empanadas
Ceviche! • Parihuela Inkawas • Arroz Chaufa
Lomo Saltado • Sudado Inkawasi

SCAN FOR MENU

SOME BASICS

Reservations:	YES
Spirits:	BEER/WINE
Parking:	LOT/STREET
Outdoor Dining:	NO

ISLAND HOUSE TAP & GRILL

5110 Ocean Boulevard
941-487-8116
islandhousetapandgrill.com

SIESTA KEY	AMERICAN	COST: $$

HOURS: Daily, 11AM to 10PM

WHAT TO EXPECT: Great Craft Beers • Fantastic Burgers & Tacos
Outdoor Patio • Local Favorite • Daily Specials

BEST BITES: Duck Fat Fries • Chicken Lollipops • Guac n' Chips
Endless Summer Salad • Carnitas Bowl
Carne Asada Tacos • Steakhouse Burger

SCAN FOR MENU

SOME BASICS

Reservations:	NO
Spirits:	BEER/WINE
Parking:	LOT
Outdoor Dining:	YES

JACK DUSTY

1111 Ritz-Carlton Drive
941-309-2266
ritzcarlton.com/en/hotels/florida/sarasota/dining/jack-dusty

DOWNTOWN	SEAFOOD	COST: $$$

HOURS: Breakfast, lunch, and dinner daily

WHAT TO EXPECT: Walking Distance To Downtown • Water View
Handmade Cocktails • OpenTable Reservations

BEST BITES: Smoked Fish Dip • Sarasota Cioppino • Lobster Roll
Jack's Fish Tacos • South Crispy Half Chicken
Panzenella Salad • Roasted Grouper

SCAN FOR MENU

SOME BASICS

Reservations:	YES
Spirits:	FULL BAR
Parking:	VALET
Outdoor Dining:	YES

VEGETARIAN OR VEGAN?
HERE ARE SARASOTA'S BEST PLACES

Vegetarian and vegan lifestyles both offer a healthy way of eating. But, as anyone who keeps either of these diets knows, dining out can sometimes be more than a challenge. I mean, how many grilled cheese sandwiches can one person consume? Don't despair. We're here to help. Sarasota has its share of options for those who choose a meat-free existence. Keep in mind that the places listed below may not be strictly vegan/veg only. But, they will offer some nice menu options.

Florence and the Spice Boys • 4990 S. Tamiami Trl. • 405-3890
THE HIGHLIGHTS: Hummus, Baba Ganoush, Falafel, and lots more. Lots of variety here. Try a Rainbow Bowl!

ionie Organic Cafe • 1444 First St. • 320-0504
THE HIGHLIGHTS: Organic, plant-based, and gluten free. They have a big menu of vegan/veg options available daily.

Lila • 1576 Main St. • 296-1042
THE HIGHLIGHTS: Named one of the best vegetarian restaurants in the country by OpenTable. Refined vegetarian cuisine.

Organic Farmer's Table • 14 N. Lemon Ave. • 362-3276
THE HIGHLIGHTS: Great for vegan/veg and those who are not. The Beet Carpaccio is great. Or try a Vegan Fiesta!

Spice Station • 14 N. Lemon Ave. • 343-2894
THE HIGHLIGHTS: Fantastic Thai cuisine. They've got a large section of vegetarian dishes on their menu. Cozy dining space.

Tandoor • 8447 Cooper Creek Blvd • 926-3077
THE HIGHLIGHTS: Indian cuisine lends itself to a vegetarian diet. There are vegetarian variations on most dishes. Since 2001.

JERSEY GIRL BAGELS
5275 University Parkway
941-388-8910
jerseygirlbagels.net

UNIVERSITY PARK	DELI	COST: $$

HOURS: Wed-Sun, 7AM to 2PM
CLOSED MONDAY & TUESDAY

WHAT TO EXPECT: NY Style Bagels • Buy One Or A Dozen!
Super Casual • Lots Of Parking • Good For A Carryout

BEST BITES: Egg Salad Sandwich • Lox & Bagel Sandwich
Black & White Cookies • Breakfast Sandwiches

SCAN FOR MENU

SOME BASICS
Reservations:	NO
Spirits:	NONE
Parking:	LOT
Outdoor Dining:	NO

JOEY D'S CHICAGO STYLE EATERY
3811 Kenny Drive*
941-378-8900
joeydsfl.com

	AMERICAN	COST: $$

HOURS: Daily, 11AM to 10PM

WHAT TO EXPECT: Chicago Style Food • Family Friendly
Multiple Locations • Super Casual

BEST BITES: World Famous Chicago Pizza • Stromboli
The Shroom Burger • Original "Chicago Style" Hot Dog
Grilled Maxwell Street Polish • Italian Beef

SCAN FOR MENU

SOME BASICS
Reservations:	NO
Spirits:	BEER/WINE
Parking:	LOT
Outdoor Dining:	YES

JPAN RESTAURANT & SUSHI BAR

3800 South Tamiami Trail (Shops at Siesta Row)*
941-954-5726
jpanrestaurant.com

SHOPS AT SIESTA ROW	JAPANESE	COST: $$

HOURS: Lunch, Mon-Fri, 11:30AM to 2PM
Mon-Sat, 5PM to 9:30PM • Sun, 5PM to 9PM

WHAT TO EXPECT: Great For A Date • Big Sushi Menu
Great Lunch Combos • OpenTable Reservations

BEST BITES: Sushi • Sashimi • Bento Boxes • Pork Dumplings
Kfc (Korean Fried Chicken) • Hamachi Chili
Ramen • Volcano Chicken

SCAN FOR MENU

SOME BASICS

Reservations:	YES
Spirits:	BEER/WINE
Parking:	LOT
Outdoor Dining:	YES

JR'S OLD PACKINGHOUSE CAFÉ

987 South Packinghouse Drive
941-371-9358
packinghousecafe.com

	AMERICAN	COST: $$

HOURS: Mon-Thur, 11AM to 9PM • Fri & Sat, 11AM to 10PM
CLOSED SUNDAY

WHAT TO EXPECT: Fun For A Date • Live Music
Great Burgers & Cuban Sandwiches

BEST BITES: Queso Burger • Cuban Sandwich OPC Style
Mediterranean Salad • Ropa Vieja • OPC Shrimp
Country Fried Chicken • Key Lime Pie

SCAN FOR MENU

SOME BASICS

Reservations:	NO
Spirits:	FULL BAR
Parking:	LOT
Outdoor Dining:	YES

KACEY'S SEAFOOD AND MORE

4904 Fruitville Road
941-378-3644
kaceysseafood.com

	SEAFOOD	COST: $$

HOURS: Mon-Sat, 11:30AM to 8PM
CLOSED SUNDAY

WHAT TO EXPECT: Casual Atmosphere Seafood • Early Dining
Lots of Parking • Good For Families and Groups

BEST BITES: Shrimp Scargot • Steamed Mussels
Seafood Gumbo • Lots Of Fresh Fish Selections
Lobster Roll • Fish Or Shrimp Tacos • Shrimp & Grits

SOME BASICS

SCAN FOR MENU

Reservations:	NO
Spirits:	BEER/WINE
Parking:	LOT
Outdoor Dining:	YES

KOJO

1289 North Palm Avenue
941-536-9717
eatkojo.com

DOWNTOWN	ASIAN	COST: $$$

HOURS: Sun-Thur, 4PM to 11PM
Fri & Sat, 4PM to 12AM

WHAT TO EXPECT: Upscale Asian Cuisine • Ramen, Sushi, & Bao Buns
Next To Palm Ave Garage • Online Reservations

BEST BITES: Wasabi Caesar Salad • Crispy Tofu Bites
Truffled Chicken Wontons • Torched Salmon Nori Taco
Bao Buns • Wagyu Skirt Steak • Sushi

SOME BASICS

SCAN FOR MENU

Reservations:	YES
Spirits:	FULL BAR
Parking:	GARAGE/STREET
Outdoor Dining:	YES

KOLUCAN

6644 Gateway Avenue
941-921-3133
kolucan.com

GULF GATE	MEXICAN	COST: $$$

HOURS: Lunch, Mon-Fri, 11AM to 3PM
Dinner, Mon-Sat, 5PM to 10PM • CLOSED SUNDAY

WHAT TO EXPECT: "Elevated Mexican Flavors" • The Frida Lounge
Upscale Dining • Great Outdoor Dining Space

BEST BITES: Elote Asado • Street Tacos • Ensalada de Berros
Tortas Planchadas • Huitlachoche Risotto
Enchiladas Divorciadas • Seasonal Red Sangria

SCAN FOR MENU

SOME BASICS

Reservations:	YES
Spirits:	FULL BAR
Parking:	LOT
Outdoor Dining:	YES

KORÊ STEAKHOUSE

1561 Lakefront Drive
941-928-5673
koresteakhouse.com

WATERSIDE PLACE	KOREAN	COST: $$$

HOURS: Open Daily, Lunch & Dinner

WHAT TO EXPECT: REAL Korean Bbq • Super Upscale Feel
Busy For Dinner • Fun For Groups

BEST BITES: Bulgogi Mandoo • Egg Souffle • Japchae Noodles
Dolsot Bibimbap • Kimchi Jjigae • Cheese Corn
Beef, Pork, Seafood, Chicken & Veggie Grilling Items

SCAN FOR MENU

SOME BASICS

Reservations:	NO
Spirits:	BEER/WINE
Parking:	STREET
Outdoor Dining:	NO

LA NORMA

5370 Gulf of Mexico Drive
941-383-6262
lanormarestaurant.com/home

LONGBOAT KEY	ITALIAN	COST: $$$

HOURS: Daily, 5PM to 9PM

WHAT TO EXPECT: Upscale Sicilian Cuisine • Cozy Atmosphere
Great For A Date • OpenTable Reservations

BEST BITES: Bruschetta Tradizionale • Giulio Cesare
Sicilian Arancini • Lasagne Tradizionali • Pizza
Veal Ravioli with Mushrooms and Truffle Oil • Tiramisu

SOME BASICS

SCAN FOR MENU

Reservations:	YES
Spirits:	BEER/WINE
Parking:	LOT
Outdoor Dining:	NO

2026 SARASOTA FOOD EVENTS

FORKS & CORKS
WHEN: January 22-26
WHAT: Sponsored by the Sarasota-Manatee Originals. Super
popular food event! Wine dinners, seminars, AND the Grand
Tasting. A must for Sarasota foodies. Tickets go very fast.
INFO: eatlikealocal.com/forksandcorks

FLORIDA WINEFEST & AUCTION
WHEN: Events throughout the year
WHAT: This charity event has been providing needed help to
local children's programs for over 30 years. The Charity Brunch &
Auction is a fantastic event! INFO: floridawinefest.org

SAVOR SARASOTA RESTAURANT WEEK
WHEN: June 1-14th
WHAT: This restaurant week spans TWO full weeks. It features
lots of popular restaurants and showcases three course menus.
INFO: savorsarasota.com

LA VIOLETTA
4837 Swift Road
941-927-8716
laviolettasrq.com

	ITALIAN	**COST: $$$**

HOURS: Tues-Sat, 4:30PM to 9PM
CLOSED SUNDAY & MONDAY

WHAT TO EXPECT: Homemade Everything! • Intimate Dining
Reservations Required • Great For A Special Occasion

BEST BITES: Animelle Di Vitello • Foie Gras • Tagliere
Schiaccia Alla Carbonara • Tartare Di Tonno
Anatra In Confit • Tortellini Di Bologna • Gelato Di Amarene

SCAN FOR MENU

SOME BASICS
Reservations:	YES
Spirits:	BEER/WINE
Parking:	LOT
Outdoor Dining:	NO

THE LAZY LOBSTER
5350 Gulf of Mexico Drive
941-383-0440
lazylobsteroflongboat.com

LONGBOAT KEY	**SEAFOOD**	**COST: $$$**

HOURS: Mon-Sat, 11AM to 9PM
CLOSED SUNDAY

WHAT TO EXPECT: Great Casual Seafood • Early Dining Menu
Lots & Lots of Lobster • Older Crowd

BEST BITES: Chilled Ahi Tuna • Lobster Scargot • Lobster Bisque
Hot Fried Chicken Salad • The Open Faced Reuben
Stuffed Shrimp "Norma" • Lobster Mac & Cheese

SCAN FOR MENU

SOME BASICS
Reservations:	YES
Spirits:	FULL BAR
Parking:	LOT
Outdoor Dining:	YES

LEFTY'S OYSTER BAR & SEAFOOD

NEW

428 North Lemon Avenue
941-954-8688
leftysoysterseafood.com

ROSEMARY DIST	SEAFOOD	COST: $$$

HOURS: Daily, 11:30AM to 10PM

WHAT TO EXPECT: Fun Upscale Atmosphere • Nice Outdoor Space
Craft Cocktails • Daily Oyster Specials • Happy Hour

BEST BITES: Oyster Shooters • Pearls & Parm • Steamed Mussels
Peel & Eat Shrimp • Frog Legs!! • Louisiana Gator Tail Bites
Maine Lobster Roll • Key West Chowder

SCAN FOR MENU

SOME BASICS
Reservations: YES
Spirits: FULL BAR
Parking: LOT
Outdoor Dining: YES

LENNY'Z PIZZA & ISLAND BAR

6645 Midnight Pass Road
941-260-8879
lennyz.pizza

SIESTA KEY	PIZZA	COST: $$

HOURS: Daily, 11AM to 11PM

WHAT TO EXPECT: Just Off SK South Bridge • Pizza & Craft Beer
Good For Families • Lots Of Parking

BEST BITES: Jalapeno Poppers • Garlic Knots
Antipasto Salad • Meatball Sub • Fried Chicken
Pizza, Pizza, Pizza! • Chocolate Chip Cookie For Dessert!

SCAN FOR MENU

SOME BASICS
Reservations: NO
Spirits: FULL BAR
Parking: LOT
Outdoor Dining: YES

SARASOTA MARKETS AND SPECIALTY STORES

A Taste of Europe • 2130 Gulf Gate Dr. • 921-9084
WHAT YOU CAN FIND THERE: Foods from twenty different European countries. Fresh deli, specialty cheeses, beer, wine, and more.

Alpine Steakhouse • 4520 S. Tamiami Trl. • 922-3797
WHAT YOU CAN FIND THERE: Meat market. Skilled butchers, super helpful. Famous for Turducken. Also, full service restaurant.

Artisan Cheese Company • 550 Central Ave. • 951-7860
WHAT YOU CAN FIND THERE: Cheese store. Hard to find small domestic dairies. Lunch menu. Classes. Knowledgeable staff.

Big Water Fish Market • 6641 Midnight Pass Rd. • 554-8101
WHAT YOU CAN FIND THERE: Fresh Florida fish. Great prepared seafood items. Just south of Siesta Key's south bridge.

The Butcher's Block • 3242 17th St. • 955-2822
WHAT YOU CAN FIND THERE: Meat market/butcher shop. Custom cuts, prime meats. Good wine selection. They have gift baskets.

Butcher's Mark • 8519 Cooper Creek Blvd. • 358-6328
WHAT YOU CAN FIND THERE: Sustainable beef. Lots of marinades and pre-marinaded meat. Charcuterie and antipasto.

The Chop Shop • 5906 Manatee Ave. W. (Bradenton) • 794-6328
WHAT YOU CAN FIND THERE: Featuring specialty cuts of meat since 1971. Full deli department. Try their homemade crab cakes!

F.L.A. DELI • 2805 Proctor Rd. • 217-5710
WHAT YOU CAN FIND THERE: European deli and market specializing in Hungarian specialties. Take home some homemade Pierogis!

Morton's Gourmet Market • 1924 S. Osprey Ave. • 955-9856
WHAT YOU CAN FIND THERE: Upscale gourmet food items including a large selection of cheeses and wine. Great deli & carryout.

SARASOTA MARKETS AND SPECIALTY STORES

Morton's Siesta Market • 205 Canal Rd. • 349-1474
WHAT YOU CAN FIND THERE: Everyday grocery items plus a good selection of prepared foods for lunch and dinner. Cold beer.

Piccolo Italian Market • 6518 Gateway Ave. • 923-2202
WHAT YOU CAN FIND THERE: Italian market. Pastas, sauces, homebaked bread, and homemade Italian sausage. Sandwiches.

Southern Steer Butcher • 4084 Bee Ridge Rd. • 706-2625
WHAT YOU CAN FIND THERE: Big selection of pre-brined beef and chicken. Full butcher shop and lots of specialty items.

Walt's Fish Market • 4144 S. Tamiami Trl. • 921-4605
WHAT YOU CAN FIND THERE: Huge selection of fresh local fish & seafood. Stone crabs when in season. Smoked mullet spread!

LIBBY'S NEIGHBORHOOD BRASSERIE
1917 South Osprey Avenue*
941-487-7300
libbysneighborhoodbrasserie.com

SOUTHSIDE VILLAGE	AMERICAN	COST: $$$

HOURS: Sun-Thur, 11AM to 9PM
Fri & Sat, 11AM to 10PM

WHAT TO EXPECT: Upscale Dining Experience • Good Wine List
Busy Bar Scene • Reservations A Must During Season

BEST BITES: Tuna Taki • Avocado Eggrolls • Kale Caesar Salad
Krabby Patty Sandwich • Meatball Smash Sandwich
Louisiana Chicken Pasta • Dr. Pepper Ribs

SCAN FOR MENU

SOME BASICS
Reservations:	YES
Spirits:	FULL BAR
Parking:	LOT/STREET
Outdoor Dining:	YES

LILA

1576 Main Street
941-296-1042
lilasrq.com

DOWNTOWN	AMERICAN	COST: $$

HOURS: Mon-Fri, 11AM to 9PM • Sat, 10:30AM to 9PM
CLOSED SUNDAY

WHAT TO EXPECT: Organic, Locally Sourced Menu • Lighter Fare
OpenTable Reservations • Lots Of Veg/Vegan Options

BEST BITES: Vegan Sushi Rolls • Roasted Yam Wedges
Red Beet, Apple, Orange Salad • Mushroom Burger
Ramen Noodle Bowl • Verlasso Salmon

SCAN FOR MENU

SOME BASICS

Reservations:	YES
Spirits:	BEER/WINE
Parking:	STREET
Outdoor Dining:	NO

LO' KEY ISLAND GRILL   `NEW`

5620 Gulf of Mexico Drive
941-387-0089
lokeylbk.com

LONGBOAT KEY	AMERICAN	COST: $$

HOURS: Daily, 2PM to 10PM

WHAT TO EXPECT: Globally Inspired Menu • Sandwiches & Burgers
Island Feel • Happy Hour Daily

BEST BITES: Tuna Poke Stack • Smoked Wings • Corn "Riblets"
Lo' Key Smash Burger • Pulled Pork Sammie
Grilled Caesar Salad • Lo' Country Boil

SCAN FOR MENU

SOME BASICS

Reservations:	NO
Spirits:	FULL BAR
Parking:	STREET
Outdoor Dining:	YES

LOBSTER POT

5157 Ocean Boulevard
941-349-2323
sarasotalobsterpot.com

SIESTA KEY	SEAFOOD	COST: $$$

HOURS: Mon-Thur, 11:30AM to 9PM • Fri & Sat, 11:30AM to 9:30PM
CLOSED SUNDAY

WHAT TO EXPECT: Great For Families • Lobster ++ • Siesta Village
Good For Kids • 25th Anniversary! (2025)

BEST BITES: Kettle of Mussels • Broiled Fiery Scallops
Portuguese Soup • Watermelon Salad • Lazy Dutchess
Alaskan King Crab • Salmon Rockefeller • Filet Mignon

SOME BASICS

SCAN FOR MENU

Reservations:	6 OR MORE
Spirits:	BEER/WINE
Parking:	VALET/STREET
Outdoor Dining:	YES

L'OPERA BAKERY & BISTRO

2336 Gulf Gate Drive
941-365-2234
1592srq.com

GULF GATE	FRENCH	COST: $$

HOURS: Daily, 7:30AM to 2PM

WHAT TO EXPECT: Delicious Baked Goods • Easy Parking
Breakfast & Lunch

BEST BITES: Croq' Madame • Lorraine Quiche
Ham & Cheese Crepe • Salad Goat Honey
Salmon Marmiton • Casslette Of Chicken

SOME BASICS

SCAN FOR MENU

Reservations:	NO
Spirits:	NONE
Parking:	LOT
Outdoor Dining:	NO

LOVELY SQUARE
6559 Gateway Avenue
941-724-2512
lovelysquareflorida.com

GULF GATE	AMERICAN	COST: $$

HOURS: Mon-Sun, 8AM to 2PM
CLOSED TUESDAY

WHAT TO EXPECT: Casual Dining Spot • Nice Selection Of Crepes
Good For Families • Easy On The Wallet

BEST BITES: Classic Eggs Benedict • Omelets & Frittatas
Morning Crepe • Banana Nut Pancakes
Greek Salad • Club B.E.L.T. • Baguette Brie Chicken

SCAN FOR MENU

SOME BASICS
Reservations:	NO
Spirits:	BEER/WINE
Parking:	LOT
Outdoor Dining:	NO

LUCKY 8   `NEW`
1812 South Osprey Avenue
941-779-5299
lucky8srq.com

SOUTHSIDE VILLAGE	CAJUN/CREOLE	COST: $$

HOURS: Mon-Sat, 11AM to 9PM
CLOSED SUNDAY

WHAT TO EXPECT: Great For A Casual Lunch or Dinner • Happy Hour
Authentic NOLA Cuisine • Lots Of Counter Seating

BEST BITES: New Orleans BBQ Shrimp • Muffuletta Sandwich
Chicken & Sausage Gumbo • Pimento Cheese!
Southern Fried Chicken Thigh • NOLA Bread Pudding

SCAN FOR MENU

SOME BASICS
Reservations:	NO
Spirits:	BEER/WINE
Parking:	STREET
Outdoor Dining:	YES

THE MABLE

2831 North Tamiami Trail
941-487-7373

NORTH TRAIL	AMERICAN	COST: $$

HOURS: Daily, 4PM to 2AM

WHAT TO EXPECT: Fantastic "Dive" Bar • Ringling College Students
Great Burger! • Lots Of Craft Beer To Choose From

BEST BITES: The Burger! • Poutine • Grilled Steak Tacos
Truffle Tater Tots • Vegetarian Chili • Potstickers
Fried Buffalo Chicken Sammy • Warm Bavarian Pretzel

SCAN FOR MENU

SOME BASICS

Reservations:	NO
Spirits:	FULL BAR
Parking:	LOT
Outdoor Dining:	YES

MAD MOE'S

106 North Tamiami Trail
941-966-9700
madmoes.com

OSPREY	AMERICAN	COST: $$

HOURS: Daily, 11AM to Close

WHAT TO EXPECT: Sports Bar Feel • A South County Fav Since 2014
Good Burger • Local Place • Super Casual

BEST BITES: Fried Pickle Chips • Avocado Egg Rolls
Chicken Cobb Salad • Tacos! • Chicago Italian Beef
Hoosier Pork Tenderloin • Pizza • Burgers!

SCAN FOR MENU

SOME BASICS

Reservations:	NO
Spirits:	FULL BAR
Parking:	LOT
Outdoor Dining:	YES

MADEMOISELLE PARIS
8527 Cooper Creek Boulevard*
941-355-2323
mademoiselleparis.com

LAKEWOOD RANCH	FRENCH	COST: $$

HOURS: Mon & Tue, 7:45AM to 5PM
Wed-Sun, 7:45AM to 9PM

WHAT TO EXPECT: Traditional French Fare • Casual European Dining
Tartines, Omelettes, And More!

BEST BITES: Tartine Gourmande • Omelettes • Quiche Lorraine
Croque Madame • Beef Burgundy • French Onion Soup
Crepes! • Profiteroles • Crême Brulée

SCAN FOR MENU

SOME BASICS

Reservations:	YES
Spirits:	BEER/WINE
Parking:	LOT
Outdoor Dining:	YES

MADFISH GRILL
4059 Cattleman Road
941-377-3474
madfishgrill.com

	SEAFOOD	COST: $$

HOURS: Mon-Sat, 11:30AM to 9PM • Sun, 11AM to 8PM
Sunday Brunch, 11AM to 2PM

WHAT TO EXPECT: Good For Families • Daily Specials
Happy Hour Bites Menu • Sunday Brunch Menu

BEST BITES: Chicken Cobb Salad • Bang Shrimp Bowl
Drunken Lobster Bisque • Blackened Grouper Sandwich
Tacos • Pan Seared Cod • Abuela's House-Made Flan

SCAN FOR MENU

SOME BASICS

Reservations:	YES
Spirits:	FULL BAR
Parking:	LOT
Outdoor Dining:	YES

MAIN BAR SANDWICH SHOP
1944 Main Street
941-955-8733
themainbar.com

DOWNTOWN	DELI	COST: $

HOURS: Mon-Sat, 10AM to 4PM
CLOSED SUNDAY

WHAT TO EXPECT: Great For Quick Lunch • Easy On The Wallet
Lively Atmosphere • Fantastic Service

BEST BITES: Famous Italian Sandwich • New Yorker Sandwich
Homemade Soups • Tuna Salad Plate • Sultan Salad
Sarasotan Wrap • Key Lime Pie

SCAN FOR MENU

SOME BASICS
Reservations:	NO
Spirits:	BEER/WINE
Parking:	STREET
Outdoor Dining:	NO

MAISON BLANCHE
2605 Gulf of Mexico Drive (Four Winds Beach Resort)
941-383-8088
themaisonblanche.com

LONGBOAT KEY	FRENCH	COST: $$$$

HOURS: Wed-Sun, 5:30PM to 9:30PM
CLOSED MONDAY & TUESDAY

WHAT TO EXPECT: Date Night! • Perfect For A Special Occasion
Excellent Service • Great Wine List • Online Reservations

BEST BITES: Wild Mushroom Raviolis With Foie Gras Sauce
Chanterelles Risotto • Tomato Tart • Red Snapper
Beef Short Ribs • Chocolate Souffle With Creme Anglaise

SCAN FOR MENU

SOME BASICS
Reservations:	YES
Spirits:	BEER/WINE
Parking:	LOT
Outdoor Dining:	NO

Louisiana Shrimp & Grits

Lucky 8
Chef Mark Majorie

This is one of the most satisfying shrimp dishes to grace the kitchens of Louisiana homes and restaurants. We utilize the shells from the shrimp to make a rich stock which is used as the base for our andouille sausage and piquillo pepper gravy. The grits are spiked with roasted poblano peppers and mascarpone cheese to bring the dish to the next level.

INGREDIENTS
½ cup andouille sausage, diced
1 shallot, minced
2 cloves garlic, minced
2 each piquillo peppers, diced
1 tablespoon fresh thyme
2 cups shrimp stock
3 cups whole peeled tomatoes
2 tablespoons unsalted butter
Juice of 1 lemon

Roasted Poblano Cheese Grits
2 cups water
2 cups milk
½ lbs butter
1 cup stone ground grits
2 cups mascarpone cheese
2 tablespoons kosher salt
1 tablespoon black pepper
2 each poblano peppers, charred, peeled, seeded, and diced

Gulf Shrimp
24 each jumbo gulf shrimp, peeled and deveined
Creole spice
2 tablespoons olive oil

METHOD

1. For the grits. In a medium sauce pot combine milk, water, and butter, then bring to a boil. Add grits and lower heat to a simmer, stirring constantly; cook for 10-12 minutes or until the grits have softened. Remove from heat and add mascarpone cheese, salt, pepper, and poblano peppers.

2. To make the sauce, start by rendering the andouille sausage until browned. Next add the butter, shallots, and garlic and slowly caramelize. Once the shallots are cooked, deglaze the pot with the shrimp stock, then add the tomatoes and thyme and allow to simmer for 45 minutes to an hour to allow the flavors to combine and the tomatoes to break down naturally. Remove the sauce from the heat and add the lemon juice and set aside until ready to serve.

3. Season the shrimp aggressively with the creole seasoning then in a hot pan, blacken the shrimp on both sides, about 2 minutes in total. Once the shrimp are seared, add a few ladles of the andouille gravy to your hot pan to meld the sauce with the blackened shrimp, simmer until the shrimp are fully cooked, then serve on top of the poblano cheese grits, garnish with some fresh green onions, and enjoy.

Welcome to Lucky 8, Sarasota's newest culinary gem from restaurateur Eddie Zaki and Chef Mark Marjorie. Inspired by the seat that brought them together, Lucky 8 celebrates the magic of connection through bold flavors, a curated wine list, and a touch of New Orleans flair. Every dish tells a story — where creativity meets comfort, and every seat might just be your lucky one. Join us for an unforgettable dining experience where luck, flavor, and friendship meet.

MALMOSTO WINE SHOP & KITCHEN

2085 Siesta Drive
941-706-1460
wineshopandkitchen.com

SOUTHGATE	ITALIAN	COST: $$$

HOURS: Mon-Sat, 5PM to Close
CLOSED SUNDAY

WHAT TO EXPECT: Cozy Indoor Dining Space • Italian Pizza
Great Hand-Curated Wine Selection • Chef Andrea Bozzolo

BEST BITES: Porketta • Boneless Short Ribs • Candele Spezzate Pasta
Seafood Paella • Pacific Blue Fin Tuna Dome
Lots Of Delicious Pizzas To Choose From

SCAN FOR MENU

SOME BASICS

Reservations:	YES
Spirits:	FULL BAR
Parking:	LOT
Outdoor Dining:	NO

BEST FISH IN Town

SARASOTA
SEAFOOD MARKETS

Big Water Fish Market • 6641 Midnight Pass Rd. • 554-8101
WHAT YOU CAN FIND THERE: Fresh Florida fish. Great prepared
seafood items. Just south of Siesta Key's south bridge.

Gulf Coast Crab & Seafood • 6986 S. Beneva Rd. • 685-2657
WHAT YOU CAN FIND THERE: Fresh out of the Gulf seafood. Stone
crab, grouper, and mahi. Catering is available.

Walt's Fish Market • 4144 S. Tamiami Trl. • 921-4605
WHAT YOU CAN FIND THERE: Huge selection of fresh local fish &
seafood. Stone crabs when in season. Smoked mullet spread!

MAR VISTA DOCKSIDE RESTAURANT & PUB
760 Broadway Street
941-383-2391
marvistadining.com

LONGBOAT KEY	AMERICAN	COST: $$

HOURS: Sun-Thur, 11:30AM to 9PM
Fri & Sat, 11:30AM to 10PM

WHAT TO EXPECT: Great For Families • Big List Of Specialty Drinks
Water View • Old Florida Feel • 14 Private Slips For Boaters

BEST BITES: Fish Dip • Beer & Old Bay Shrimp • Crab Cake Trio
Seafood Gumbo • Cobia Burger • Seafood Paella
Chef's Boil Pot • Coconut Cake

SCAN FOR MENU

SOME BASICS
Reservations:	NO
Spirits:	FULL BAR
Parking:	LOT
Outdoor Dining:	YES

MARCELLO'S RISTORANTE
4155 South Tamiami Trail
941-921-6794
marcellosarasota.com

SOUTH TRAIL	ITALIAN	COST: $$$

HOURS: Tue-Sat, 5:30PM to 9PM
CLOSED SUNDAY & MONDAY

WHAT TO EXPECT: Nice Wine List • Chef Driven Italian Cuisine
Small & Intimate Dining Experience

BEST BITES: Grilled Octopus • Beef Carpaccio • Lamb Ragu
Braised Beef Short Ribs • Diver Sea Scallops
Hudson Valley Duck Breast • Tiramisu • Cannoli

SCAN FOR INFO

SOME BASICS
Reservations:	YES
Spirits:	BEER/WINE
Parking:	LOT
Outdoor Dining:	NO

MARINA JACK'S

2 Marina Plaza
941-365-4232
marinajacks.com

DOWNTOWN	SEAFOOD	COST: $$$

HOURS: Sun-Thur, 11AM to 9PM
Fri & Sat, 11AM to 10PM

WHAT TO EXPECT: Water View • Dinner Cruises • Live Music
Nice Wine List • Live Music • Outdoor Lounge

BEST BITES: Filet Mignon Center Cut • Prawn Martini
Charcuterie Board • Sherry Crab Bisque • Mahi Francaise
Pan Seared Scallops • Bouillabaisse • Lump Crab Cakes

SCAN FOR MENU

SOME BASICS
Reservations:	YES
Spirits:	FULL BAR
Parking:	VALET/LOT
Outdoor Dining:	YES

MATTISON'S CITY GRILLE

1 North Lemon Avenue
941-330-0440
mattisons.com

DOWNTOWN	AMERICAN	COST: $$

HOURS: Lunch - Daily, 11AM to 3PM
Dinner - Daily, 4:30PM to 10PM

WHAT TO EXPECT: Great For A Date • Downtown Meet-Up Spot
Live Music • Great Bar Service • Happy Hour Daily

BEST BITES: Tuna Poke Tower • NE Clam Chowder • Shakshuka
Niman Ranch Reuben • Brick Oven Pizza!
Seafood Gumbo • Grouper Piccata • Key Lime Pie

SCAN FOR MENU

SOME BASICS
Reservations:	YES
Spirits:	FULL BAR
Parking:	STREET
Outdoor Dining:	YES

MATTISON'S FORTY ONE

7275 South Tamiami Trail
941-921-3400
mattisons.com

SOUTH TRAIL	AMERICAN	COST: $$

HOURS: Mon-Thur, 11:30AM to 9PM • Fri, 11:30AM to 10PM
Sat, 4:30PM to 10PM • CLOSED SUNDAY

WHAT TO EXPECT: Large Wine List • Brunch • Good Value
Online Reservations • Happy Hour Menu

BEST BITES: Artichokes Esther-Style • Wedge Salad • Pork Belly
Forty-One Burger • Rack Of Lamb • Fish & Chips
Maple Leaf Farms Duck • Thai Soba Noodle Bowl

SOME BASICS

SCAN FOR MENU

Reservations:	YES
Spirits:	FULL BAR
Parking:	LOT
Outdoor Dining:	NO

MEAN DEANS LOCAL KITCHEN

6059 26th Street W.
941-251-5435
meandeanslocalkitchen.com

BRADENTON	AMERICAN	COST: $$$

HOURS: Sun-Thur, 11AM to 9PM
Fri & Sat, 11AM to 10PM

WHAT TO EXPECT: Catering Available
Locally Sourced Ingredients • Good Wine List

BEST BITES: Deconstructed Goat Cheese Bruschetta
Calamari & Peppers • Candied Bacon Bleu
Pork Osso Bucco • Lobster Lasagna • Brooklyn Ice Cream

SOME BASICS

SCAN FOR MENU

Reservations:	YES
Spirits:	FULL BAR
Parking:	LOT
Outdoor Dining:	NO

MEDITERRANEO

1970 Main Street
941-365-4122
mediterraneorest.com

DOWNTOWN	ITALIAN	COST: $$

HOURS: Lunch, Mon-Fri, 11:30AM to 2:30PM
Dinner, Daily from 5:30PM

WHAT TO EXPECT: Pizza • Good Wine List • Italian Specialties
Online Reservations • Private Party Dining Space

BEST BITES: Carpaccio Rucola • Mista Salad • Gamberi Salad
Minestrone Soup • Linguine Mare • Pollo Milanese
Paninis • Le Pizze Classiche • Profiteroles

SCAN FOR MENU

SOME BASICS

Reservations:	YES
Spirits:	FULL BAR
Parking:	STREET/GARAGE
Outdoor Dining:	YES

MICHAEL'S ON EAST

1212 East Avenue South
941-366-0007
bestfood.com

MIDTOWN PLAZA	AMERICAN	COST: $$$

HOURS: Tue-Thur, 5PM to 8:30PM • Fri & Sat, 5PM to 9PM
CLOSED SUNDAY AND MONDAY

WHAT TO EXPECT: Piano Lounge • Catering • Fine Dining
OpenTable Reservations • AAA Four Diamond Award

BEST BITES: Lobster & Escargots • Mussels Marinière
East Avenue Caesar • Colony Snapper • Duck Two-Ways
Michael's Famous Bowtie Pasta • Brownie Ice Cream Stack

SCAN FOR MENU

SOME BASICS

Reservations:	YES
Spirits:	FULL BAR
Parking:	VALET
Outdoor Dining:	YES

MICHELLE'S BROWN BAG CAFÉ

630 North Orange Avenue
941-365-5858
michellesbrownbagcafe.com

DOWNTOWN	DELI	COST: $

HOURS: Mon-Fri, 9AM to 2PM
CLOSED SATURDAY & SUNDAY

WHAT TO EXPECT: Quick Lunch • Easy On The Wallet
Great Meet-Up Spot • Super Casual

BEST BITES: Longboat Brie Sandwich • Bayfront Tuna Sandwich
Farmer's Market Salad • Paninis • Lox & Bagel
Turkey Reuben • Half Sandwich + Soup!

SOME BASICS

SCAN FOR MENU

Reservations:	NO
Spirits:	BEER/WINE
Parking:	GARAGE/STREET
Outdoor Dining:	NO

MIGUEL'S

6631 Midnight Pass Road
941-349-4024
miguelsrestaurant.net

SIESTA KEY	FRENCH	COST: $$$

HOURS: Dinner, Daily from 4PM
Early Dinner Menu, 4PM to 6PM

WHAT TO EXPECT: Good Wine List • Quiet Atmosphere
Good Early Dining Menu • Nice For A Date

BEST BITES: Les Escargot Bourgogne • Steak Tartare
Sopa De Ajo • Les Fruits De Mer • Moules Normandy
Le Chateaubriand Bouquetiere • Le Veau Piccata

SOME BASICS

SCAN FOR MENU

Reservations:	YES
Spirits:	FULL BAR
Parking:	LOT
Outdoor Dining:	NO

MILLIE'S CAFÉ
3900 Clark Road
941-923-4054
eatatmillies.com

AMERICAN	**COST: $$**

HOURS: Tue-Sun, 7AM to 2:30PM
CLOSED MONDAY

WHAT TO EXPECT: Since 1988 • Breakfast & Lunch
Daily Specials • Soup of the Day!

BEST BITES: Eggs Benedict • Spinach and Feta Cheese Omelet
German Apple Pancakes • French Crepes
Russian Blintzes • Reuben Sandwich • Millie's Patty Melt

SCAN FOR INFO

SOME BASICS
Reservations:	NO
Spirits:	NONE
Parking:	LOT
Outdoor Dining:	NO

MIRNA'S CUBAN CUISINE
2901 North Tamiami Trail
941-316-9793
mirnascubancuisine.com

NORTH TRAIL	**CUBAN**	**COST: $**

HOURS: Tue-Thur,11AM to 8PM • Fri & Sat, 11AM to 9PM
Sun, 11AM to 6PM • CLOSED MONDAY

WHAT TO EXPECT: Authentic Cuban Cuisine • Casual Atmosphere
Scratch Kitchen • Super Affordable

BEST BITES: Papas Rellenas • Ropa Vieja • Vaca Frita
Cuban Roast Pork • Churrasco Steak • Arroz Con Pollo
Cuban Sandwich • Pan Con Leche • Flan

SCAN FOR MENU

SOME BASICS
Reservations:	NO
Spirits:	NONE
Parking:	LOT
Outdoor Dining:	NO

MOLLY'S RESTAURANT & PUB

1562 Main Street
941-366-7711
eviesonline.com/location/mollys-pub

DOWNTOWN	IRISH	COST: $$

HOURS: Tues-Sat, 4PM to 10PM
CLOSED SUNDAY & MONDAY

WHAT TO EXPECT: Fun Pub Atmosphere • Downtown Location
Special Events • Great After Work Meetup Spot

BEST BITES: Shepherd's Pie • Bangers & Mash • Reuben
Cobb Salad • Hot Ham & Cheese • Deviled Eggs
Salmon BLT • Molly's Burger • Grilled Wings

SOME BASICS

SCAN FOR MENU

Reservations:	NO
Spirits:	FULL BAR
Parking:	STREET/GARAGE
Outdoor Dining:	YES

Keep Up With Your Favorite Sarasota Restaurants

FOLLOW, LIKE & SUBSCRIBE
DineSarasota

MONK'S STEAMER BAR

6690 Superior Avenue
941-927-3388
monkssteamerbar.com

GULF GATE	SEAFOOD	COST: $$

HOURS: Mon-Thur, 3PM to 12AM • Fri & Sat, 12PM to 1AM
Sunday, 12PM to 12AM

WHAT TO EXPECT: Steamed Everything! • Dive Bar/Great Food
Locals Favorite • Late Night Menu

BEST BITES: Seafood Bisque • Oysters Monkafeller • Mussels
Cajun Crawfish • Peel N Eat Shrimp • Oyster Shooters!

SCAN FOR MENU

SOME BASICS

Reservations:	NO
Spirits:	FULL BAR
Parking:	STREET/LOT
Outdoor Dining:	NO

MOUTHOLE SMASHBURGERS

2637 Mall Drive
941-746-4653

GULF GATE	AMERICAN	COST: $$

HOURS: Lunch: Tue-Sat, 12PM to 3PM • Dinner: Tue-Sat, 5PM to 8PM
CLOSED SUNDAY & MONDAY

WHAT TO EXPECT: Super Casual • Great Smash-Style Burgers!
BBQ • Great for Carryout • Say HI To Ray & Nikki

BEST BITES: The O.G. Burger • The Gouda Smash
The Sloppy Egg • Loaded Mac Bowl • Brisket Sammie
Banana Pudding • The Porker Sandwich

SCAN FOR MENU

SOME BASICS

Reservations:	NO
Spirits:	BEER/WINE
Parking:	LOT/STREET
Outdoor Dining:	NO

MY VILLAGE PUB (MVP)
5200 Ocean Boulevard
941-777-6787
mvpsiestakey.com

SIESTA KEY	AMERICAN	COST: $$

HOURS: Daily, 11AM to Close

WHAT TO EXPECT: Great for Any Game • Lots of Outdoor Seating
Heart Of SK Village • 20+ Draft Beers • Friendly Bar Staff

BEST BITES: Avocado Egg Rolls • BLT Dip • Boom Boom Shrimp
Tacos! • Tuna Poke Bowl • MVP Double Mac Cheeseburger
Grouper Reuben • Flatbreads • Ballpark Fries!!

SCAN FOR MENU

SOME BASICS
Reservations:	NO
Spirits:	FULL BAR
Parking:	STREET
Outdoor Dining:	YES

---

99 BOTTLES TAPROOM
1445 Second Street
941-487-7874
99bottles.net

DOWNTOWN	BEER	COST: $$

HOURS: Mon-Thur, 3PM to 11PM
Fri-Sun, 9AM to 12AM

WHAT TO EXPECT: Big City Feel • Knowledgeable Bar Staff
"Pop-Up" Dining Events • Great For An After Work Beer

BEST BITES: NY Bagel Brunch (Weekends)
Bagel Sandwiches • Best Craft Beer Selection in Sarasota

SCAN FOR MENU

SOME BASICS
Reservations:	NO
Spirits:	BEER/WINE
Parking:	STREET/GARAGE
Outdoor Dining:	YES

WORLD FAMOUS COCONUT SHRIMP

Tommy Bahama

INGREDIENTS

Sauce:
One 9-oz jar mango chutney, such as Major Grey's
1 Tbsp Dijon mustard
1 Tbsp mango nectar or pineapple juice

Batter:
¾ cup seafood fry mix or unbleached all-purpose flour
1 cup lager beer
5 large egg yolks
4 tsp sugar
1¼ tsp kosher salt
½ tsp freshly ground black pepper

Frying:
Vegetable oil, for deep-frying
½ cup unbleached, all-purpose flour
¾ cup sweetened coconut flour
16 extra-jumbo (16 to 20 count) shrimp, peeled and deveined, tall intact

METHOD

For the Sauce:
Purée all the ingredients in a blender. Transfer to a small bowl, cover, and set aside.

For the Batter:
Whisk all the ingredients together in a large bowl. Let stand for 10 to 15 minutes.

Position a rack in the center of the oven and preheat the oven to 200°F. Pour 2" oil into a large, deep saucepan and heat over high heat to 350°F on a deep-fry thermometer.

Spread the flour in a shallow bowl. Spread the coconut in a second bowl. Place a wire rack on a large, rimmed baking sheet. One at a time, toss the shrimp in the flour, then in the batter, letting the excess batter drip back into the bowl. Roll the shrimp in the coconut to coat evenly. Transfer to a platter.

In batches, without crowding, deep-fry the shrimp, turning them halfway through frying, until golden brown, about 2½ minutes. Using a wire spider or a slotted spoon, transfer the shrimp to the wire rack and keep warm in the oven while frying the rest.

To serve, pour the sauce into a small serving bowl, heap the shrimp on a platter, and serve with the sauce as a dip.

SERVES 4-6

Tommy Bahama has always communicated its brand message of relaxation and the luxury of leisure time through a distinctive restaurant and retail experience. The Tommy Bahama Restaurant, Bar & Store in Sarasota is the brand's second restaurant/retail location, first opened in 1996. Today the location is together again, re-opening in September 2025 after years of separation and storm damage. The new location in St. Armands Circle returns with delicious, island-inspired cuisine; locally-sourced seafood and produce are used for a variety of signature dishes; handcrafted cocktails feature premium spirits, fresh squeezed juices and house made syrups; and seasonal menus throughout the year reflect the bounty of Southwest Florida and local culinary traditions.

Join the other 18,000+
Follow us on Facebook!

dineSarasota

18K followers · 588 following

NAKED FARMER

215 North Cattlemen Road
941-870-9412
eatnakedfarmer.com

UTC	AMERICAN	COST: $$

HOURS: Mon-Sat, 11AM to 9:30PM
Sunday, 11:30AM to 9PM

WHAT TO EXPECT: Mini Chain • "Unmessed-With Deliciousness"
Farm To Table Menu • Vegan/Veg Options

BEST BITES: Backyard BBQ Chicken Plate • Classic Naked
Steak & Mushroom Plate • High Protein Plate
Faroe Island Salmon Plate • Farmer's Panzanella

SCAN FOR MENU

SOME BASICS
Reservations:	NO
Spirits:	NONE
Parking:	LOT
Outdoor Dining:	NO

NAMO IZAKAYA

1439 Main Street
941-362-3332
namoizakaya.com

DOWNTOWN	ASIAN	COST: $$

HOURS: Daily, 11AM to 10PM

WHAT TO EXPECT: Casual Japanese Cuisine • Main St. Location
Small But Mighty Menu

BEST BITES: Sweet Corn Cheese • Namo Fried Chicken
Hijiki Seaweed Salad • Tonkotsu Ramen
Salmon Teriyaki • Unagi • Creamy Curry

SCAN FOR MENU

SOME BASICS
Reservations:	YES
Spirits:	BEER/WINE
Parking:	STREET
Outdoor Dining:	YES

NAPULÈ RISTORANTE ITALIANO

7129 South Tamiami Trail
941-556-9639
napulesarasota.com

SOUTH TRAIL	ITALIAN	COST: $$$

HOURS: Mon-Thur, 11:30AM to 9:30PM
Fri & Sat, 11:30AM to 10:30PM • CLOSED SUNDAY

WHAT TO EXPECT: Upscale Italian Dining • Great Wood Oven Pizza
Very Busy In Season • Vibrant Atmosphere

BEST BITES: Salumeria • Burrata • Bufala Salad • Fresella Salad
Trio di Bruschette • Polipetti Alla Luciana
Saltimbocca Di Vitello Alla Romana • Pizza!

SOME BASICS

SCAN FOR MENU

Reservations:	YES
Spirits:	FULL BAR
Parking:	LOT
Outdoor Dining:	YES

NEW PASS GRILL & BAIT SHOP

1505 Ken Thompson Parkway
941-388-3050
newpassgrill.com

CITY ISLAND	AMERICAN	COST: $

HOURS: Daily, 7AM to 7PM

WHAT TO EXPECT: Casual Dining • Water View • More Than Burgers
Bait & Tackle Shop • A "Landmark" Since 1929

BEST BITES: Breakfast! • NE Clam Chowder • BLT
Hot Dog Or Polish Sausage • New Pass Burgers
Fried Chicken Sandwich • Fish N Chips • Ice Cream Bar!

SOME BASICS

SCAN FOR MENU

Reservations:	NO
Spirits:	BEER/WINE
Parking:	LOT
Outdoor Dining:	YES

SARASOTA
UPSCALE CHAIN DINING

Sarasota has a ton of great independently owned and operated restaurants. And, that's mostly what this dining book is all about. But, as with any decent sized city, we've got our share of quality, upscale chain dining options, too.

We've taken the time to put together a list of some of our favorites. Just like the main section of the book, we didn't have the space to list them all. So, we curated a collection of the ones we think will give you a consistent and favorable dining experience.

We've tried to include a little bit of everything here for you. Some steakhouses, sushi, deli, and even pizza. You'll recognize most of the names, I'm sure. There's something here for everyone.

Bonefish Grill • 3971 S. Tamiami Trl. • 924-9090
WHAT TO EXPECT: Upscale casual place to meet up with friends and enjoy drinks or dinner. Lots of seafood options. ($$)

Brio Tuscan Grille • 190 University Town Center Dr. • 702-9102
WHAT TO EXPECT: Italian cuisine. UTC. Online reservations. Lively atmosphere. Good for groups. ($$$)

Cooper's Hawk • 3130 Fruitville Commons Blvd. • 263-8100
WHAT TO EXPECT: Steaks, seafood, much more. Fantastic wine selection. Modern, casual dining. ($$$)

Capital Grille • 180 University Town Center Dr. • 256-3647
WHAT TO EXPECT: Big city steakhouse. Very upscale dining experience. Reservations/OpenTable. Private dining. ($$$$)

Chart House • 201 Gulf of Mexico Dr. • 383-5593
WHAT TO EXPECT: Fresh seafood. Nice gulf view. Always outstanding service. Classic upscale dining experience. ($$$)

SARASOTA UPSCALE CHAIN DINING

Cheesecake Factory • 130 University Town Center Dr. • 256-3760
WHAT TO EXPECT: 200+ menu choices. Super large portions. Happy Hour. Catering. Very busy dining atmosphere. ($$$)

CW Prime • 1601 Gulf of Mexico Dr • 233-9036
WHAT TO EXPECT: St. Regis LBK Hotel. Fine dining experience. Steaks and chops cooked on the Josper grill. ($$$$)

Fleming's Prime Steakhouse • 2001 Siesta Dr. • 358-9463
WHAT TO EXPECT: Super high quality steaks + service. Private dining. "Fleming's 100" wines. Happy Hour. ($$$$)

Hyde Park Steakhouse • 35 S. Lemon Ave. • 366-7788
WHAT TO EXPECT: Busy downtown location. Valet parking. Popular Happy Hour. "Early Nights" menu. Private dining. ($$$$)

Ocean Prime • 501 Quay Commons • 404-1024
WHAT TO EXPECT: Prime steaks, chops, and seafood. Top flight service. Elegant dining experience. ($$$$)

P.F. Chang's Bistro • 766 S. Osprey Ave. • 296-6002
WHAT TO EXPECT: "Farm to Wok" Asian cuisine. Large menu. Busy, vibrant atmosphere. Good for groups. Online reservations. ($$$)

Rodizio Brazilian Steakhouse • 5911 Fruitville Rd. • 260-8445
WHAT TO EXPECT: Brazilian steakhouse experience. Rotisserie grilled meats. Tableside service. Large gourmet salad bar. ($$$)

Ruth's Chris Steakhouse • 6700 S. Tamiami Trl. • 942-8982
WHAT TO EXPECT: Exceptional service. Older dining crowd. Large selection of USDA prime steaks. Great wine list. ($$$$)

Seasons 52 • 170 University Town Center Dr. • 702-5652
WHAT TO EXPECT: Seasonal menu selections. 52 wines by the glass. UTC Mall. Group dining options. Great service. ($$$)

Sophie's • 120 University Town Center Dr. • 444-3077
WHAT TO EXPECT: UTC inside Saks Fifth Avenue. "Ladies" lunch spot. Intimate dining experience. Great for private parties. ($$$)

131 MAIN

NEW

6608 University Parkway
941-394-0131
131-main.com/lakewood-ranch

LAKEWOOD RANCH	AMERICAN	COST: $$$

HOURS: Sun-Thur, 11AM to 9PM
Fri & Sat, 11AM to 9:30PM

WHAT TO EXPECT: Upscale Casual • Good LWR Meet Up Spot
Online Reservations • Cashless Payments Only

BEST BITES: Ahi Tuna Stack • Classic Cheeseburger
North Carolina Rainbow Trout • Danish Baby Back Ribs
Barrel Cut Filet Mignon • Deviled Eggs

SCAN FOR MENU

SOME BASICS

Reservations:	YES
Spirits:	FULL BAR
Parking:	LOT
Outdoor Dining:	NO

OASIS CAFÉ & BAKERY

3542 South Osprey Avenue
941-957-1214
theoasiscafe.net

	AMERICAN	COST: $$

HOURS: Tue-Fri, 7AM to 2PM • Sat & Sun, 8AM to 1:30PM
CLOSED MONDAY

WHAT TO EXPECT: Breakfast & Lunch • Casual Dining
Great Daily Specials • Homemade Pastries & Baked Goods

BEST BITES: Eggs Benedict • Cheese Blintzes • Lox & Bagel
Italian Scramble • Blackened Basa Reuben
Soup & Salad Combo • Siesta Sister Wrap

SCAN FOR MENU

SOME BASICS

Reservations:	NO
Spirits:	BEER/WINE
Parking:	LOT
Outdoor Dining:	YES

THE OLD SALTY DOG

5023 Ocean Boulevard*
941-349-0158
theoldsaltydog.com

SIESTA KEY	AMERICAN	COST: $$

HOURS: Daily, 11AM to 9PM

WHAT TO EXPECT: Locals Love It • Vacation Feel • Cold Beer
As Seen On TV! • Great For Families

BEST BITES: Hand-Cut Onion Rings • Peel N Eat Shrimp
NE Clam Chowder • The Famous "Salty Dog"
Grouper Reuben • Firecracker Wrap • Fish N Chips

SOME BASICS

SCAN FOR MENU

Reservations:	NO
Spirits:	FULL BAR
Parking:	STREET
Outdoor Dining:	YES

O'LEARY'S TIKI BAR & GRILL

5 Bayfront Drive
941-953-7505
olearystikibar.com

DOWNTOWN	AMERICAN	COST: $$

HOURS: Sun-Thur, 8AM to 10PM
Fri & Sat, 8AM to 11PM

WHAT TO EXPECT: Live Music • Beach Bar • Cold Beer
Great Views • Watersports Rentals • Super Relaxed

BEST BITES: Mozzarella Sticks • Peel & Eat Shrimp
Rachel Sandwich • Soft Shell Crab Sandwich • Mahi Tacos
The Works Burger • Ultimate Margarita

SOME BASICS

SCAN FOR MENU

Reservations:	NO
Spirits:	FULL BAR
Parking:	LOT
Outdoor Dining:	YES

OPHELIA'S ON THE BAY

9105 Midnight Pass Road
941-349-2212
opheliasonthebay.net

SIESTA KEY	AMERICAN	COST: $$$

HOURS: Dinner Nightly, 5PM to 10PM

WHAT TO EXPECT: Great For A Date • Nice Water View
Good Wine List • OpenTable Reservations

BEST BITES: Thai Oishii Shrimp Cocktail • Escargot Ophelia
Vermont Creamery Chevre & Chioggia Beets
Key West Yellowtail Snapper • Thomas Farms Rack Of Lamb

SCAN FOR MENU

SOME BASICS

Reservations:	YES
Spirits:	FULL BAR
Parking:	VALET
Outdoor Dining:	YES

ORIGIN CRAFT BEER & PIZZA CAFÉ

1837 Hillview Street*
941-316-9222
originpizzacafe.com

SOUTHSIDE VILLAGE	PIZZA	COST: $$

HOURS: Sun-Thur, 11AM to 1AM
Fri & Sat, 11AM to 2AM

WHAT TO EXPECT: Neighborhood Feel • Open Late • Friendly Staff
Local Favorite • Five Sarasota Area Locations • Craft Beer

BEST BITES: Great Wings! • Pizza! • Quinoa Tab'bouleh Salad
Stromboli • Mediterranean Platter • Meatballs

SCAN FOR MENU

SOME BASICS

Reservations:	NO
Spirits:	BEER/WINE
Parking:	LOT/STREET
Outdoor Dining:	YES

OSTERIA 500
1580 Lakefront Drive
941-866-8962
osteria500.com

WATERSIDE PLACE	ITALIAN	COST: $$$

HOURS: Sun-Thur, 11AM to 9:30PM
Fri & Sat, 11AM to 10:30PM

WHAT TO EXPECT: Casual Italian Cuisine • New Waterside Place
No Reservations - First Come, First Served

BEST BITES: Caprese Rivistata • Guazzetto Napoletano
Linguini Cozze E Vongole • Margherita Pizza
Branzino Mediterranero • Profiterole

SCAN FOR MENU

SOME BASICS
Reservations:	NO
Spirits:	FULL BAR
Parking:	LOT
Outdoor Dining:	NO

ORTYGIA
1418 13th Street W.
941-741-8646
ortygiarestaurant.com

BRADENTON	EUROPEAN	COST: $$$

HOURS: Wed-Sat, 5PM to 8PM
CLOSED SUNDAY, MONDAY & TUESDAY

WHAT TO EXPECT: Intimate Dining Experience • Chef Driven Menu
Nice Outdoor Dining Space • Village Of The Arts

BEST BITES: Mushroom Pate • Veal Piccata • Timballo
"Seafood Of The Week" • Dark Chocolate Pate
Pasta La Norma • Locally Made Gelato

SCAN FOR MENU

SOME BASICS
Reservations:	YES
Spirits:	BEER/WINE
Parking:	STREET
Outdoor Dining:	YES

OWEN'S FISH CAMP
516 Burns Court*
941-951-6936
owensfishcamp.com

BURNS COURT	SEAFOOD	COST: $$

HOURS: Daily, 4PM to 9PM

WHAT TO EXPECT: Fun Dining Experience • Good For Families
Busy In Season • Parking Can Be A Challenge

BEST BITES: Deviled Eggs • Garlic Snail With Chorizo
Maryland Spiced Shrimp • Low Country Boil
Crispy Chicken • Spicy Jambalaya • Shrimp & Grits

SCAN FOR MENU

SOME BASICS
Reservations:	NO
Spirits:	FULL BAR
Parking:	STREET/LOT
Outdoor Dining:	YES

PACIFIC RIM
1859 Hillview Street
941-330-8071
pacrimsrq.com

SOUTHSIDE VILLAGE	ASIAN	COST: $$

HOURS: Mon-Fri, 11:30AM to 2PM • Mon-Thur, 4:30PM to 9PM
Fri & Sat, 4:30PM to 10PM • Sun, 4:30PM to 9PM

WHAT TO EXPECT: Fun Dining Experience • Sushi & More
Parking Usually Available • Happy Hour

BEST BITES: Crispy Spring Roll • Tuna Carpaccio • Sushi
Sashimi • Drunken Noodles • Wok Dishes • Red Curry
Teriyaki Chicken • Shrimp Tempura • Green Tea Ice Cream

SCAN FOR MENU

SOME BASICS
Reservations:	YES
Spirits:	FULL BAR
Parking:	LOT/STREET
Outdoor Dining:	YES

PALM AVENUE DELI
1297 North Palm Avenue
941-263-3742
palmavenuedeli.com

DOWNTOWN	DELI	COST: $$

HOURS: Daily, 7AM to 11PM

WHAT TO EXPECT: NY Style Deli • Bustling REAL Deli Feel
QR Table Side Ordering • Palm Ave Garage = Easy Parking

BEST BITES: Matzo Brei • Egg Creams • Burnt Ends Pastrami Hash
Potato Latkes • Palm Avenue Cobb • Matzo Ball Soup
Corned Beef Sandwiches • Stuffed Cabbage • Reubens

SCAN FOR MENU

SOME BASICS
Reservations:	NO
Spirits:	BEER/WINE
Parking:	STREET/GARAGE
Outdoor Dining:	YES

THE PARROT PATIO BAR & GRILL
3602 Webber Street
941-952-3352
theparrotpatiobar.com

	AMERICAN	COST: $$

HOURS: Sun-Thur, 11:30AM to 11PM
Fri & Sat, 11AM to 12AM

WHAT TO EXPECT: Very Casual • Sports Bar Feel • Live Music
NFL Football Package • Good For Groups

BEST BITES: Smoked Fish Dip • Coconut Shrimp • Buffalo Wings
Buffalo Shrimp • Southwest Taco Salad • Seared Ahi Tuna
Pizza! • Beef On Weck • Grouper Reuben • Burgers

SCAN FOR MENU

SOME BASICS
Reservations:	NO
Spirits:	FULL BAR
Parking:	LOT
Outdoor Dining:	YES

PASTRY ART
1512 Main Street
941-955-7545
pastryartcafe.com

DOWNTOWN	AMERICAN	COST: $$

HOURS: Mon-Sat, 7AM to 4PM
Sun, 8AM to 3PM

WHAT TO EXPECT: Great For A Coffee Date • In Business 30+ Years
Busy Weekend Spot • Casual Downtown Hangout

BEST BITES: Avocado Toast • Lox & Bagel • Steak & Egg Sandwich
Reuben Sandwich • Beet Salad • Rainbow Salad
Turkey Avocado BLT • Homemade Soup

SCAN FOR MENU

SOME BASICS

Reservations:	NO
Spirits:	BEER/WINE
Parking:	STREET
Outdoor Dining:	YES

PATRICK'S 1481
1481 Main Street
941-955-1481
patricks1481.com

DOWNTOWN	AMERICAN	COST: $$

HOURS: Mon-Thur, 11AM to 9PM • Fri, 11AM to 10PM
Sat, 10AM to 10PM • Sun, 10AM to 9PM

WHAT TO EXPECT: Downtown Since 1985 • Local Favorite
Good Craft Beer Selection • Known For Their Burgers

BEST BITES: Spinach & Artichoke Dip • Roasted Beet Salad
1481 Salad • Award Winning Burgers • Scampi
Fish N Chips • Yankee Pot Roast • Key Lime Pie

SCAN FOR MENU

SOME BASICS

Reservations:	YES
Spirits:	FULL BAR
Parking:	STREET/VALET
Outdoor Dining:	YES

PAZZO ON ORANGE

481 North Orange Avenue
941-364-4682
pazzoonorange.com

ROSEMARY DIST	ITALIAN	COST: $$$

HOURS: Mon-Fri, 12PM to 9PM • Sat, 4PM to 10PM
Sun, 5PM to 9PM

WHAT TO EXPECT: Lunch Sandwiches • Pizza
Great Outdoor Dining Space • Homemade Italian Cuisine

BEST BITES: Classic Italian Sandwich • Pasta Fagioli
Meatball Salad • Braised Short Rib Ravoli
Chevelatta Sausage Platter • Andrew's Cheesecake

SOME BASICS

SCAN FOR MENU

Reservations:	YES
Spirits:	FULL BAR
Parking:	STREET
Outdoor Dining:	YES

PHILLIPPI CREEK OYSTER BAR

5353 South Tamiami Trail
941-925-4444
creekseafood.com

SOUTH TRAIL	SEAFOOD	COST: $$

HOURS: Daily 11AM to 9:30PM
Happy Hour, 3PM to 5:30PM

WHAT TO EXPECT: Great For Families • Water View • Casual Dining
Busy During Season • Good For Kids

BEST BITES: Oysters Rockefeller • Fried Smelt • Florida Cobb Salad
Jumbo Shrimp Cocktail • Oysters! • "Norfolks"
Steamed Pots • Seafood Paella • Root Beer Float

SOME BASICS

SCAN FOR MENU

Reservations:	NO
Spirits:	FULL BAR
Parking:	LOT
Outdoor Dining:	YES

PHO CALI

1578 Main Street
941-955-2683
phocalisarasota.com

DOWNTOWN	VIETNAMESE	COST: $$

HOURS: Mon-Thur, 11AM to 9PM • Fri & Sat, 11AM to 9:30PM
CLOSED SUNDAY

WHAT TO EXPECT: Great Service • Casual Dining
Easy On The Wallet • Good For Families • Noodle Bowls!

BEST BITES: Pork & Shrimp Vietnamese Pancake • Roasted Quail
Daily Specials • Pho Noodle Bowls • Noodle Stir Fry
Rice Vermicelli Noodle Bowls • Roasted Duck

SCAN FOR INFO

SOME BASICS

Reservations:	NO
Spirits:	BEER/WINE
Parking:	STREET
Outdoor Dining:	NO

PICCOLO ITALIAN MARKET & DELI

6518 Gateway Avenue
941-923-2202
piccolomarket.com

GULF GATE	ITALIAN	COST: $

HOURS: Tue-Sat, 11AM to 5PM
CLOSED SUNDAY & MONDAY

WHAT TO EXPECT: Great For A Quick Lunch • Italian Market
Super Casual • Delicious Sandwiches • Catering Available

BEST BITES: Italian Chopped Salad • The Godfather Sandwich
Meatball Parm Sandwich • Pizza! • Pasta Marinara
Chicken Piccata • Cannoli

SCAN FOR MENU

SOME BASICS

Reservations:	NO
Spirits:	NONE
Parking:	LOT
Outdoor Dining:	NO

Food Trucks are popular. And, just like every other great food community, we've got our share roaming the streets. Here's a little basic info to help you navigate through the maze of local mobile dining options. These are a few of our favorites!

DAN APIZZ' MAN NEW HAVEN STYLE
What They Serve: New Haven Style pizza! This is a fantastic version of this regional style pie. Get it!
Where You Can Find Them: Sun King Brewing Wed-Fri. Sarasota Farmer's Market on Saturdays

CURRYWURST TRUCK SRQ
What They Serve: Authentic German street food. Kielbasa Roll, Currywurst, Polski Roll, Veggie Wurst Roll.
Where You Can Find Them:
Various stops around the Sarasota area.
Info at: facebook.com/currywursttrucksrq

HAMLET'S EATERY
What They Serve: Tacos and slider boxes. Both meat and vegan options are available.
Where You Can Find Them:
The Bazaar on Apricot & Lime
Info at: hamletseatery.com

THE MAINE LINE
What They Serve: Lobster a bunch of different ways. Also Clam "Chowdah." Try a Lobstah Grilled Cheese!
Where You Can Find Them: Various locations around the Sarasota area. Check their website for details.
Info at: themaineline.net

PIE ON MAIN
1507 Main Street
941-217-6370
pieonmain.com

DOWNTOWN	PIZZA	COST: $$

HOURS: Sun-Thur, 11AM to 12AM
Fri & Sat, 11AM to 2AM

WHAT TO EXPECT: Late Night Dining • Pizza, Pizza!
Great For A Game • Casual Downtown Lunch

BEST BITES: Garlic Knots • Truffle Fries • Meatballs
BBQ Chicken Pizza • Island Supreme Pizza
Strawberry & Pecan Salad • Wings! • Subs!

SCAN FOR MENU

SOME BASICS

Reservations:	NO
Spirits:	FULL BAR
Parking:	STREET
Outdoor Dining:	NO

PIER 22
1200 1st Avenue West
941-748-8087
pier22dining.com

BRADENTON	SEAFOOD	COST: $$$

HOURS: Mon-Thur, 11:30AM to 10PM • Fri, 11:30AM to 10:30PM
Sat, 8AM to 10:30PM • Sun, 8AM to 10PM

WHAT TO EXPECT: Great For A Date • Water View • Good Wine List
Happy Hour • Weekend Brunch

BEST BITES: Asian Lettuce Wrap • Poutine • Fish Tacos
Flatbreads • NE Clam Chowder • Cobb Salad
Grouper Piccata • New York Cheesecake

SCAN FOR MENU

SOME BASICS

Reservations:	YES
Spirits:	FULL BAR
Parking:	LOT
Outdoor Dining:	YES

PIGFISH

5377 McIntosh Road (Calusa Brewing)
941-777-5220
pig.fish

AMERICAN	COST: $$

HOURS: Mon & Tues, 4PM to 9PM • Wed-Sat, 12PM to 9PM
Sunday, 12PM to 6PM

WHAT TO EXPECT: It's In A Brewery! • Lots Of Parking
"Gastropub" • Sustainably Sourced Ingredients

BEST BITES: The Pigfish Sandwich • Blistered Shishitos
Calusa Beer Cheese • Fish & Chips • Sausage Platter
B.L.T.E. • Taco Tuesdays!

SOME BASICS

SCAN FOR MENU

Reservations:	NO
Spirits:	BEER/WINE
Parking:	LOT
Outdoor Dining:	YES

POP'S SUNSET GRILL

112 Circuit Road (ICW Marker 10 by boat)
941-488-3177
popssunsetgrill.com

NOKOMIS	SEAFOOD	COST: $$

HOURS: Daily, 8AM to 10PM

WHAT TO EXPECT: Online "Waitlist" • Serving Breakfast!
Water View • Vacation Atmosphere • Great For Families

BEST BITES: Sunrise Benedict • Shrimp Cocktail • NE Clam Chowder
Pizza! • Raw Bar • Coconut Shrimp • Burgers
Grouper Reuben • Chocolate Toffee Mousse Cake

SOME BASICS

SCAN FOR MENU

Reservations:	NO
Spirits:	FULL BAR
Parking:	LOT
Outdoor Dining:	YES

PORK ROLL PETE'S

4657 Cortez Road W.
941-896-3333
prpbagels.com

BRADENTON	DELI	COST: $

HOURS: Mon-Fri, 6AM to 2PM
Sat & Sun, 6AM to 3PM

WHAT TO EXPECT: Super Casual • Great For A Carry Out
Lunch & Breakfast Only • Super Friendly Counter Staff

BEST BITES: Jersey Boy Bagel Sandwich • Italiano Sandwich
Milanese Sandwich • Italian Sausage Sandwich
Aunt Joyce's Macaroni Salad • Yoo-hoo Chocolate Drink

SCAN FOR MENU

SOME BASICS

Reservations:	NO
Spirits:	NONE
Parking:	LOT
Outdoor Dining:	YES

POST KITCHEN & BAR

8433 Cooper Creek Boulevard
941-259-4850
postkitchenandbar.com

COOPER CREEK	AMERICAN	COST: $$$

HOURS: Mon-Thur, 11AM to 9PM • Fri & Sat, 11AM to 10PM
Sunday, 11AM to 8:30PM

WHAT TO EXPECT: Modern American Cuisine • Upscale Atmosphere
Fresh, Local Ingredients • Lots Of Parking

BEST BITES: Raw Bar • French Onion Gratine • Tuna Tartare
Lobster Mango Salad • Truffle Pasta • Post Burger
Braised Short Rib • NY Strip Steak • Sticky Ribs

SCAN FOR MENU

SOME BASICS

Reservations:	YES
Spirits:	FULL BAR
Parking:	LOT
Outdoor Dining:	NO

PRIME SERIOUS STEAK

133 South Tamiami Trail
941-837-8325
primeserioussteak.com

VENICE	STEAKHOUSE	COST: $$$

HOURS: Mon-Fri, 4PM to 10PM • Sat, 12PM to 10PM
Sunday, 12PM to 9PM

WHAT TO EXPECT: Steakhouse Atmosphere • Happy Hour Daily
Great For A Special Occasion

BEST BITES: Loaded Potato Pancakes• Shrimp Cocktail
"Pub Style" Onion Soup • Black Grouper • Kansas City Strip
Surf and Turf • Creamed Spinach

SCAN FOR MENU

SOME BASICS

Reservations:	YES
Spirits:	FULL BAR
Parking:	LOT
Outdoor Dining:	NO

RED PLUM ASIAN BISTRO & SUSHI BAR

7119 South Tamiami Trail
941-554-8816
redplumsarasota.com

SOUTH TRAIL	ASIAN	COST: $$$

HOURS: Lunch & Dinner, Wed-Mon
CLOSED TUESDAY

WHAT TO EXPECT: Casual Sushi • Good For A Group
Creative Rolls • Lots Of Parking

BEST BITES: Sushi & Sashimi Lunch Specials • Pork Belly Bao
Steamed Shrimp Shumai • Sushi Combos
Spicy Maki Combo • Sashimi Tartar

SCAN FOR MENU

SOME BASICS

Reservations:	YES
Spirits:	BEER/WINE
Parking:	LOT
Outdoor Dining:	NO

Lefty's Fresh Seafood Ceviche

Chef Raul Rodriguez

INGREDIENTS
1½ lb. Gulf grouper or mahi, cut into small pieces
1 small red pepper, diced
1 small yellow pepper, diced
½ red onion, diced
½ cup fresh cilantro
13 ripe Limes
Two oranges
Salt & Pepper to taste

METHOD
Marinate the onions, peppers and citrus with fish. Toss in the cilantro.

Refrigerate. The citrus marinade will 'ceviche cure' the fish as the flavors are absorbed.

Serve with mucho amor!

NOTE - Choose the freshest fish that you can find for this dish.

Lefty's Oyster & Seafood Bar offers the revival of coastal seafood in a rustic, comfortable atmosphere. Our made-to-order fare & innovative cocktails will chart your course to sharing a good meal with friends & family. Join us to experience the watershed moments when hospitality gives its all and the gems of the sea live up to their reputation. "I love oysters. It's like kissing the sea on the lips." – Leon-Paul Fargue"
For more information call (941) 954-8688.
Or leftysoysterseafood.com.

RENDEZ-VOUS FRENCH BAKERY
5336 Clark Road
941-924-1234
rendezvoussarasota.com

PALMER CROSSING	FRENCH	COST: $$

HOURS: Tues-Sat, 7:30AM to 3PM • Sunday, 8AM to 3PM
CLOSED MONDAY

WHAT TO EXPECT: Real French Bakery • Super Casual
The Pastries Are Fantastic! • Catering Available

BEST BITES: La Quiche Lorraine • Le Croque Madame
French Omelettes • French Onion Soup
Baguette Sandwiches • La Nicoise Salad

SOME BASICS
SCAN FOR MENU

Reservations:	NO
Spirits:	NONE
Parking:	LOT
Outdoor Dining:	NO

RICK'S FRENCH BISTRO
2177 Siesta Drive
941-957-0533
ricksfrenchbistro.com

SOUTHGATE	FRENCH	COST: $$$

HOURS: Wed-Sat, 5PM to 9PM
CLOSED SUNDAY, MONDAY & TUESDAY

WHAT TO EXPECT: Initmate Dining Experience • Limited Seating
Authentic French Cuisine • Lots Of Parking

BEST BITES: Soupe a l'Oignon Gratinee • Saumon Fume Sur Toasts
Steak au Poivre • Crevettes a la Marseillaise
Boeuf Bourguignon • Chocolate Mousse

SOME BASICS
SCAN FOR MENU

Reservations:	YES
Spirits:	BEER/WINE
Parking:	LOT
Outdoor Dining:	NO

RINGSIDE (CIRQUE ST. ARMANDS) NEW

233 Benjamin Franklin Drive
941-413-5992
opalcollection.com/cirque-st-armands/restaurants/ringside

LIDO KEY	AMERICAN	COST: $$$

HOURS: Daily, 7AM to 10PM

WHAT TO EXPECT: American Coastal Cuisine • Online Reservations
Breakfast, Lunch & Dinner • Cirque St. Armands Hotel

BEST BITES: Smoked Salmon Toast • Lobster Benedict
Smoked Gulf Coast Shrimp • St. Armands Cobb
Maine Lobster Bisque • Oven-Roasted Lamb Rack

SCAN FOR MENU

SOME BASICS

Reservations:	YES
Spirits:	FULLBAR
Parking:	LOT
Outdoor Dining:	NO

RIVERHOUSE REEF & GRILL

995 Riverside Drive
941-729-0616
riverhousefl.com

PALMETTO	SEAFOOD	COST: $$$

HOURS: Mon-Thur, 11:30AM to 9PM • Fri, 11:30AM to 10PM
Sat, 11AM to 10PM • Sun, 11AM to 9PM

WHAT TO EXPECT: Waterfront Dining • Happy Hour
Sunday Brunch • Regatta Pointe Marina

BEST BITES: Blue Crab Dip • Oysters • Island Time Salad
Lobster Corn Chowder • Grouper Tacos
Burgers • Lobster Roll • Lobster Pot Pie

SCAN FOR MENU

SOME BASICS

Reservations:	YES
Spirits:	FULL BAR
Parking:	LOT
Outdoor Dining:	YES

ROMANSQ
6670 Superior Avenue
941-237-8742
romansq.com

GULF GATE	PIZZA	COST: $$

HOURS: Wed-Sat, 12PM to 8PM • Sun, 12PM to 4PM
CLOSED MONDAY & TUESDAY

WHAT TO EXPECT: Roman Style Pizza! • Limited Seating
Great For A Carry Out

BEST BITES: Margherita • Salsiccia Friarielli • Cacio Pepe
Prosciutto Crudo • Salsiccia Rosmarino

SCAN FOR MENU

SOME BASICS
Reservations:	NO
Spirits:	NONE
Parking:	LOT
Outdoor Dining:	NO

ROSE & IVY
1296 1st Street
941-343-2122
roseivysrq.com

DOWNTOWN	PAN-ASIAN	COST: $$$

HOURS: Sun-Thur, 4PM to 12AM
Fri & Sat, 4PM to 1AM

WHAT TO EXPECT: Upscale Casual Atmosphere • Steaks + Sushi
Historic Downtown Locale • Great Craft Cocktails

BEST BITES: Salmon Carpaccio • Rose & Ivy Salad
Dim Sum • Shrimp & Scallops • Korean Bone-In Pork Chop
Organic Miso Soup • Specialty Rolls

SCAN FOR MENU

SOME BASICS
Reservations:	YES
Spirits:	FULL BAR
Parking:	STREET
Outdoor Dining:	YES

ROSEBUD'S STEAKHOUSE & SEAFOOD
2215 South Tamiami Trail
941-918-8771
rosebudssarasota.com

OSPREY	STEAKHOUSE	COST: $$$

HOURS: Tues-Sun, 4PM to 10PM
CLOSED MONDAY

WHAT TO EXPECT: Early Bird Dining • Private Dining Room
Aged, Hand Cut, Angus Steaks • Established 1995

BEST BITES: Oysters On The Half Shell • Escargot • Duck Wings
Prime Rib • Surf & Turf • Center Cut Pork Chops
BBQ Ribs • Sea Bass "Crab Louie" • Key Lime Pie

SCAN FOR MENU

SOME BASICS

Reservations:	YES
Spirits:	FULL BAR
Parking:	LOT
Outdoor Dining:	NO

ROSEMARY AND THYME
511 North Orange Avenue
941-955-7600
therosemarysarasota.com

ROSEMARY DIST	AMERICAN	COST: $$$

HOURS: Tue-Sun, 4:30PM to 9PM
Sunday Brunch, 9AM to 2PM

WHAT TO EXPECT: Upscale, But Casual • Fantastic Sunday Brunch
Great Appetizers • Don't Forget Dessert

BEST BITES: Belgian Waffle • Greek Quiche • Avocado Toast
Bermuda Fish Cake Benedict • Escargots
Pistachio-Dusted Salmon • Steak Frites

SCAN FOR INFO

SOME BASICS

Reservations:	YES
Spirits:	FULL BAR
Parking:	STREET
Outdoor Dining:	NO

SAGE
1216 First Street
941-445-5660
sagesrq.com

DOWNTOWN	AMERICAN	COST: $$$

HOURS: Tues-Thur, 5PM to 10PM • Fri & Sat, 5PM to 11PM
CLOSED SUNDAY & MONDAY

WHAT TO EXPECT: Upscale Dining • Private Event Space
Online Reservations • Rooftop Bar Is Great For A Date

BEST BITES: Seasonal Menu • Bison Short Rib • House Made Rigatoni
Portuguese Mussels • Maple Leak Farms Duck
Beyond S'Mores • Creme Brulee

SOME BASICS
SCAN FOR MENU

Reservations:	YES
Spirits:	FULL BAR
Parking:	LOT/STREET
Outdoor Dining:	YES

SAMBA BRAZILIAN STEAKHOUSE
6115 South Tamiami Trail
941-586-2040

`NEW`

SOUTH TRAIL	BRAZILIAN	COST: $$$

HOURS: Mon, Tue, Thu, Sun 12PM to 9PM
Fri & Sat, 12PM to 12AM

WHAT TO EXPECT: Brazilian Steakhouse • Great For A Date
Fun With A Group • Live Brazilian Music

BEST BITES: Brazilian Croquets • Pork Belly with Yucca
Brazilian Empanadas • Filet Mignon Gorgonzola
Beef Ribs • Whole Tilapia • Brazilian Coconut Pudding

SOME BASICS
SCAN FOR MENU

Reservations:	YES
Spirits:	FULL BAR
Parking:	LOT
Outdoor Dining:	NO

SAMURAI JAPANESE FUSION

1936 Hillview Street
941-777-7707
samurai-fl.com

SOUTHSIDE VILLAGE	ASIAN	COST: $$

HOURS: Mon-Thur, 11AM to 10PM • Fri & Sat, 11AM to 11PM
Sun, 12PM to 10PM

WHAT TO EXPECT: Casual Sushi • Southside Village Location
Great For Groups • Lunch Specials

BEST BITES: Chicken Lettuce Wrap • Takoyaki
Sashimi • Duck Bao Rolls • Boom Boom Prawns
Sushi Rolls • Hibachi Menu

SCAN FOR MENU

SOME BASICS

Reservations:	YES
Spirits:	NONE
Parking:	STREET
Outdoor Dining:	YES

SANDBAR SEAFOOD & SPIRITS

100 Spring Avenue
941-778-0444
sandbardining.com

ANNA MARIA	SEAFOOD	COST: $$

HOURS: Mon-Thur, 11AM to 9PM
Fri-Sun, 11AM to 10PM

WHAT TO EXPECT: Waterfront Dining • Old Florida Charm
Great For Locals & Visitors • History Back to 1911!

BEST BITES: Raw Bar • Crab Cakes • Roasted Beet Salad
Stuffed Shrimp • Shrimp & Grits • Crabby Grouper
Hogfish Sandwich • New England Lobster Roll

SCAN FOR MENU

SOME BASICS

Reservations:	NO
Spirits:	FULL BAR
Parking:	LOT
Outdoor Dining:	YES

SCHNITZEL KITCHEN
6521 Superior Avenue
941-922-9299
sites.google.com/view/schnitzelsrq/home

GULF GATE	GERMAN	COST: $$

HOURS: Tues-Sun, 4PM to 9PM
CLOSED SUNDAY & MONDAY

WHAT TO EXPECT: Casual Ethnic Cuisine • Homemade Dishes
Big German Beer Selection

BEST BITES: Kinder Sausage • Potato Pancakes • Schweinhaxe
Wiener Schnitzel • Chicken Paprika • Gulash
Schweinebraten • Spätzle • Apple Strudel

SOME BASICS
SCAN FOR MENU

Reservations:	YES
Spirits:	BEER & WINE
Parking:	LOT/STREET
Outdoor Dining:	NO

SELVA GRILL
1345 Main Street*
941-362-4427
selvagrill.com

DOWNTOWN	PERUVIAN	COST: $$$

HOURS: Sun-Thur, 5PM to 11PM
Fri & Sat, 5PM to 1AM

WHAT TO EXPECT: Great For A Date • Great Ceviche
Late Night & Happy Hour Menus • Also A UTC Location

BEST BITES: Wahoo Ceviche • Selva Wild Ceviche • Tuna Tiradito
Empanadas • Selva's Crab Cake • Atun a la Parilla
Selva's Famous Skirt Steak • Malbec Braised Short Ribs

SOME BASICS
SCAN FOR MENU

Reservations:	YES
Spirits:	FULL BAR
Parking:	STREET/PALM GARAGE
Outdoor Dining:	YES

Craft beer, brew pubs, and full on local breweries. Sarasota is not immune to the small batch beer craze. As a matter of fact, we've got some damn good beer craftsmen right here in town. Oh, and along with these local artisans are some great places to down a few unique brews. Here's a list of some of our local favorites. - Cheers!

SARASOTA BREWERIES & BREWPUBS

3 CAR GARAGE BREWING
8405 Heritage Green Way
Bradenton, FL 34212
941-741-8877
3cargaragebrewing.com

BIG TOP BREWING
3045 Fruitville Commons Boulevard
Sarasota, FL 34240
941-225-8438
bigtopbrewing.com

BREW LIFE BREWING
5765 South Beneva Road
Sarasota, FL 34233
941-952-3831
brewlifebrewing.com

CALUSA BREWING
5377 McIntosh Road
Sarasota, FL 34233
941-922-8150
calusabrewing.com

GOOD LIQUID BREWING
1570 Lakefront Drive
Sarasota, FL 34240
941-238-6466
goodliquidbrewingcompany.com

MOTORWORKS BREWING
1014 9th Street W
Bradenton, FL 34205
941-567-6218
motorworksbrewing.com

SUN KING BREWING
1215 Mango Avenue
Sarasota, FL 34237
941-893-3940
sunkingbrewing.com

SARASOTA BEER BARS

99 BOTTLES
1445 2nd Street
Sarasota, FL 34236
941-487-7874
99bottles.net

SHAMROCK PUB
2257 Ringling Boulevard
Sarasota, FL 34237
941-952-1730
shamrocksarasota.com

Please Drink Responsibly

SERVING SPOON

1825 South Osprey Avenue
941-388-7235
theservingspoonsarasota.com

SOUTHSIDE VILLAGE	AMERICAN	COST: $$

HOURS: Mon-Sat, 7AM to 2:30PM
Sunday, 8AM to 1:30PM

WHAT TO EXPECT: Breakfast & Lunch • Fresh Pressed Juices
Good For A Group • Southside Village Is Busy!

BEST BITES: Morning Protein Bowl • Hillview Scramble
Avocado Toast • Skillets! • Caribbean Salad
TMC Wrap • Pressed "Cuban" Spoon Style

SCAN FOR MENU

SOME BASICS

Reservations:	NO
Spirits:	NONE
Parking:	STREET
Outdoor Dining:	NO

SHAKESPEARE'S CRAFT BEER & GASTRO PUB

3550 South Osprey Avenue
941-364-5938
shakespearesenglishpub.com

	BRITISH	COST: $$

HOURS: Daily, 11:30AM to 9PM

WHAT TO EXPECT: Great For After Work Meet-Up • Good For Lunch
Fantastic Burger • Traditional English Fare

BEST BITES: Black & Blue Burger • Tomato & Feta Salad
Caramelized Onion & Brie Burger • Cottage Pie
Bangers & Mash • English Fish & Chips

SCAN FOR MENU

SOME BASICS

Reservations:	NO
Spirits:	BEER/WINE
Parking:	LOT
Outdoor Dining:	YES

SHANER'S PIZZA
6500 Superior Avenue
941-927-2708
shanerspizza.com

GULF GATE	BRITISH	COST: $$

HOURS: Mon-Sat, 11:30AM to 9PM
Sunday, 3:30PM to 9PM

WHAT TO EXPECT: Cracker Crust Pizza • Since 1991!
Sports Bar Feel • Maybe You'll See Shane Rawley!

BEST BITES: Homemade Mozzarella Sticks • Buratta Caprese
Caesar Salad • Wings! • Bronx Meatball Hoagie
Pizza! • Chicken Parm • Stuffed Cheese Shells

SOME BASICS
SCAN FOR MENU

Reservations:	NO
Spirits:	BEER/WINE
Parking:	LOT/STREET
Outdoor Dining:	NO

SHARKY'S ON THE PIER
1600 Harbor Drive South
941-488-1456
sharkysonthepier.com

VENICE	AMERICAN	COST: $$$

HOURS: Sun-Thur, 11:30AM to 10PM
Fri & Sat, 11:30AM to 11PM

WHAT TO EXPECT: Live Music • On The Beach • Very "Florida"
Voted Florida's Best Beach Bar ('13, '18, '19)

BEST BITES: NE Clam Chowder • Cabo Calamari • Sharky's Rice Bowl
Spiced Seafood Nachos • Boathouse Salad
Island Jambalaya • Captain Sharky's Platter

SOME BASICS
SCAN FOR MENU

Reservations:	YES
Spirits:	FULL BAR
Parking:	LOT
Outdoor Dining:	YES

SHEBEEN IRISH PUB & KITCHEN
6607 Gateway Avenue
941-952-3070

GULF GATE	IRISH	COST: $$

HOURS: Tues-Thur, 4PM to 8PM • Fri & Sat, 4PM to 9PM
Sun, 4PM to 8PM • CLOSED MONDAY

WHAT TO EXPECT: Authentic Irish Pub • LIVE Music
Great For Groups • Grab A Guinness

BEST BITES: Chicken Pot Pie • Corned Beef And Cabbage
Leek & Mushroom Croquettes • Bangers & Mash
Fish & Chips • Shepherd's Pie

SCAN FOR INFO

SOME BASICS
Reservations:	NO
Spirits:	BEER/WINE
Parking:	LOT
Outdoor Dining:	YES

SHORE
800 Broadway Street
941-259-4600
dineshore.com/location/shore-longboat-key

LONGBOAT KEY	AMERICAN	COST: $$$

HOURS: Daily, 11AM to 9PM

WHAT TO EXPECT: Online Reservations • Busy During Season
Good Wine List • Happy Hour • Upscale Island Feel

BEST BITES: Tuna Tartare • Lobster, Shrimp & Crab Cobb Salad
Vegan Kale 'Caesar' • Shore Burger
Grilled Branzino • Pasta Al Fresco • Ahi Tuna Mignon

SCAN FOR MENU

SOME BASICS
Reservations:	YES
Spirits:	FULL BAR
Parking:	STREET
Outdoor Dining:	YES

SIEGFRIED'S RESTAURANT
1869 Fruitville Road
941-330-9330
siegfrieds-restaurant.com

DOWNTOWN	GERMAN	COST: $$

HOURS: Wed-Sun, 4PM to 10PM
CLOSED MONDAY & TUESDAY

WHAT TO EXPECT: Casual Dining • Family Owned
Authentic German Cuisine • German Beer-Garden

BEST BITES: Wiener Schnitzel • Sauerbraten
Rheinische Reibekuchen • Leberkase Platter
Spatzle • German Schnitzel

SOME BASICS

SCAN FOR MENU

Reservations:	YES
Spirits:	BEER/WINE
Parking:	LOT/STREET
Outdoor Dining:	YES

SIESTA KEY OYSTER BAR (SKOB)

5238 Ocean Boulevard
941-346-5443
skob.com

SIESTA KEY	AMERICAN	COST: $$

HOURS: Mon-Thur, 11AM to 11PM • Fri & Sat, 11AM to 12AM
Sun, 9AM to 11PM

WHAT TO EXPECT: Vacation Atmosphere • Live Music Daily
Sunday Brunch • Oyster Happy Hour • Busy In Season

BEST BITES: Tuna Poke Bites • Wings! • Crab Cakes
The SKOB Salad • Seafood Big Boil • Big Boy Mac N Cheese
Chicken N Waffles • Blackened Grouper Reuben

SCAN FOR MENU

SOME BASICS
Reservations:	NO
Spirits:	FULL BAR
Parking:	LOT/STREET
Outdoor Dining:	YES

SO FRENCH CAFE

6280 Lockwood Ridge Road
941-388-8936
sofrenchcafe.com

	FRENCH	COST: $$

HOURS: Tues-Sat, 10AM to 5PM
CLOSED SUNDAY & MONDAY

WHAT TO EXPECT: Casual French Fare • Organic Ingredients
Special Event Nights Including Music & Dancing

BEST BITES: Savory & Sweet Crepes (Buckwheat Crepes Available)
Baguette Sandwiches • Smoothies • Blue Cheese Salad
Coffees & Teas

SCAN FOR MENU

SOME BASICS
Reservations:	NO
Spirits:	BEER/WINE
Parking:	LOT
Outdoor Dining:	NO

SIMON'S COFFEE HOUSE
5900 South Tamiami Trail
941-926-7151
simonstogo.com

SOUTH TRAIL	AMERICAN	COST: $$

HOURS: Mon-Sat, 8AM to 3PM
Sunday Brunch, 10AM to 2PM

WHAT TO EXPECT: Great Vegan/Veg Selections • Juice & Coffee Bar
Great For A Quick Meetup • Craft Beer & Wine

BEST BITES: Garden Panini Meal • Patriot Oatmeal
Tropical Blast Smoothie • Farmhouse Skillet • Kitesurfer
Spanakopita • Turkey Club Crepes • Hummus Plate

SOME BASICS
SCAN FOR MENU

Reservations:	NO
Spirits:	BEER/WINE
Parking:	LOT
Outdoor Dining:	YES

SOUTHSIDE DELI
1825 Hillview Street
941-330-9302
southsidedelisarasota.com

SOUTHSIDE VILLAGE	DELI	COST: $$

HOURS: Mon-Fri, 7AM to 6PM • Sat, 7AM to4PM
CLOSED SUNDAY

WHAT TO EXPECT: Since 1999! • Local Favorite • Great Soups!
Super Casual Dining • Drive Up Pickup Window

BEST BITES: Breakfast Omelets • Egg & Cheese Breakfast Sandwich
Scones • Southside Waldorf • Tuna Plate • Village Club
Chicken Gyro • Lunch Combos! • Half Sandwiches

SOME BASICS
SCAN FOR MENU

Reservations:	NO
Spirits:	NONE
Parking:	STREET
Outdoor Dining:	YES

A Beginner's Guide To
BOURBON & RYE

By Broc Smith, Owner - Dive Wine & Spirits

Bourbon and rye, much like wine, can't be boxed into a single category. From soft wheated bourbons to fiery barrel-proof ryes, each style offers a unique lens into American whiskey-making. Whether you enjoy yours neat, with a splash of water, or in a cocktail, exploring these categories ensures there's always something new to discover.

Bourbon and rye, contain worlds of complexity that go beyond the terms "sweet" or "strong." Both are rooted in American history, with bourbon born in Kentucky and rye linked to the whiskey traditions of the Northeast. Each bottle is a balance of grain, oak, time, and craftsmanship.

To make sense of this category, I like to divide whiskey into five main components:

BODY – Bourbon and rye range from light and approachable to full-bodied and chewy. A whiskey's mouthfeel is shaped by its mash bill, proof, and aging.

SWEETNESS – Bourbon leans sweeter thanks to its corn base, while rye delivers drier, spicier flavors. Barrel char adds caramel and vanilla tones that increase the impression of sweetness.

SPICE/TANNIN – Similar to red wine tannins, the spice and grip of whiskey comes from both rye grain and oak tannins. High rye styles are naturally more bold, while wheated bourbons are softer.

Acidity/Freshness – While whiskey doesn't have "acidity" like wine, freshness is perceived in mint, citrus, and herbal notes, often more prominent in younger or rye-forward whiskeys.

PROOF – Alcohol by Volume (ABV) plays a big role. Low-proof bourbons are softer and easy-drinking, while barrel-proof releases can be fiery, oily, or mouth-coating, requiring a splash of water to open them up.
Like wine, balance is everything. A bourbon or rye where sweetness, spice, oak, and alcohol are in harmony offers the most pleasure and is easier to sip neat, on the rocks, or pair with food.

BOURBON STYLES

Classic Kentucky Straight Bourbon

Characteristics: Caramel, Vanilla, Oak, Baking Spices, Honey

Regions: Primarily Kentucky, but also Tennessee, Indiana, and emerging distillers nationwide.

This is bourbon in its truest form: at least 51% corn, aged in new charred oak barrels. The style is approachable yet rich, offering classic notes of vanilla, caramel, and baking spice. Best enjoyed with BBQ, fried chicken, or pecan pie.

Easily Found: Michters, Elijah Craig Small Batch, Four Roses Single Barrel

Buy It If You Find It: Old Forester Single Barrel, Buffalo Trace, Russell's Reserve Single Rickhouse, Eagle Rare Unicorn: George T. Stagg, Michters 10 Year, Colonel E.H. Taylor Barrel Proof

Wheated Bourbon

Characteristics: Soft, Sweet Bread, Toffee, Red Fruit, Creamy Oak

Regions: Kentucky and beyond.

Instead of rye, wheat is the secondary grain in the mash bill. This creates a smoother, rounder whiskey with less spice and more pastry-like sweetness. Wheated bourbons have seen a surge in popularity due to the scarcity and pursuit of Pappy Van Vinkle. Excellent with roasted turkey, cornbread, or apple desserts.

Easily Found: Maker's Mark, Willett Pot Still Small Batch

Buy It If You Find It: Old Fitzgerald 7 yr Bottled-in-Bond, Larceny Barrel Proof

Unicorn: Pappy Van Winkle 15 yr, Old Fitzgerald Decanter Bottle (9-19 yr)

High-Rye Bourbon

Characteristics: Cinnamon, Black Pepper, Mint, Dark Chocolate.

Regions: Kentucky, Indiana, and craft distilleries across the U.S.

High-rye bourbons use a larger percentage of rye grain, giving them extra spice and brightness. They pair beautifully with grilled steaks, peppery sauces, and sharp cheeses.

Easily found: Four Roses Small Batch Select, Old

Grand-Dad Bonded, Basil Hayden

Buy It If You Find It: Blanton's, Elmer T. Lee, Wilderness Trail Single Barrel, Smoke Wagon Straight Bourbon, Peerless Double Oaked

Unicorn: Old Forester Birthday Bourbon, King of Kentucky, Rockhill Farms, Four Roses Small Batch Limited Edition

Barrel Proof/Cask Strength Bourbon

Characteristics: Intense Caramel, Dark Fruit, Oak, Leather, Tobacco

Regions: Widely produced in Kentucky and by craft distillers.

These bourbons are bottled straight from the barrel without dilution, often between 110–130 proof. They showcase concentrated flavors and benefit from a splash of water or ice cube to reveal their complexity. Pair with slow-braised meats, chocolate desserts, or a cigar.

Suggested Bottles: Most producers bottle a barrel proof/cask proof in some form. At Dive Wine & Spirits/Liquor Locker, we travel to distilleries to select the finest barrels of whiskey we can find. The distilleries bottle and custom label our selections for retail sale and bar use.

RYE WHISKEY STYLES

Classic Rye Whiskey (95% Rye Mash Bill)

Characteristics: Black Pepper, Dill, Mint, Eucalyptus, Citrus Peel

Regions: Indiana (MGP), Kentucky, New York, and Pennsylvania.

Rye whiskey, America's original spirit, is sharper and more herbaceous than bourbon. It is fantastic in cocktails like the Manhattan or Old Fashioned, or paired with smoked salmon and pastrami.

Easily Found: Rittenhouse Rye Bottled-in-Bond, Sazerac Rye, Whistle Pig 10 Year

Buy It If You Find It: Whistle Pig Boss Hog, High West Midwinter Night's Dram

Unicorn: Thomas H. Handy, Sazerac 18 Yr

Maryland-Style Rye (Sweeter & Softer)

Characteristics: Caramel, Honey, Light Spice, Baking Bread

Regions: Maryland, some Kentucky brands revive the style.

This historic style balances rye spice with a gentler sweetness, thanks to more corn in the mash bill. It's an easy sipper and versatile with lighter foods like roast chicken or crab cakes.

Suggested Bottles: Pikesville Rye, Sagamore Spirit, Leopold Bros.

High-Proof & Single Barrel Rye

Characteristics: Clove, Anise, Leather, Tobacco, Bold Oak

Regions: Kentucky, Indiana, craft distillers nationwide These ryes offer powerful spice and oak-driven depth. With their punchy profile, they shine with charcuterie, strong cheeses, or dark chocolate.

Easily Found: Wild Turkey 101 Rye, Willett Family Estate Rye, Michter's Single Barrel Rye

Buy It If You Find It: Willett Family Estate Single Barrel Store Pick Rye, Michter's Barrel Proof Rye

Unicorn: Parker's Heritage Heavy Char Rye

Beyond sipping, bourbon has earned a place in the kitchen as a flavor enhancer for both savory and sweet dishes. Its natural notes of caramel, vanilla, oak, and spice make it ideal for deglazing pans to create rich sauces, marinating meats like pork or beef, or adding depth to barbecue glazes.

On the sweeter side, bourbon pairs beautifully with chocolate, pecans, and caramel, showing up in classics like bourbon pecan pie, bread pudding, and even ice cream. When cooking, a splash is usually enough—the alcohol burns off, leaving behind layers of complexity that elevate everyday recipes into something memorable. If you'd like an additional resource, I recommend Chef Edward Lee's book *Bourbon Land*.

Broc Smith moved to Sarasota in 2010 to open Liquor Locker. He has since opened Dive Wine & Spirits with a combination of 2 cocktail bars and a pop up kitchen. Not one to rest, he has opened Dive Charters for catering, & DoughBoy Swift. The final place, Maso, opens late 2025. Enjoying travel, he likes to bring back flavors from all over the world to pair with his fine wines, tequilas, and bourbon.

SPEAKS CLAM BAR

29 North Boulevard of Presidents*
941-232-7633
speaksclambar.com

ST. ARMANDS	SEAFOOD	COST: $$$

HOURS: Mon-Thur, 11AM to 10PM • Fri & Sat, 11AM to11PM
Sun, 12PM to 10PM

WHAT TO EXPECT: Clams! • "Italian" Clam Bar • Upscale But Casual
Gluten Free Menu • Good For Groups

BEST BITES: Raw Bar • Shrimp Arancini • Drunken Pei Mussels
Lobster Bisque • Maine Lobster Roll • Shrimp & Clam Bowl
Lasagna Bolognese • Chicken Marsala

SCAN FOR MENU

SOME BASICS

Reservations:	YES
Spirits:	FULL BAR
Parking:	GARAGE/STREET
Outdoor Dining:	YES

SPEARFISH GRILLE

1265 Old Stickney Point Road
941-349-1971
spearfishgrille.com

SIESTA KEY	SEAFOOD	COST: $$

HOURS: Daily, 11AM to 10PM

WHAT TO EXPECT: Super Casual • Island Feel
Fresh Seafood • Good For Families • Live Music

BEST BITES: Crispy Fried Grouper Cheeks • Tuna Poke
Fresh Gulf Hogfish • Cheesy Gulf Shrimp And Grits
Gulf Shrimp Po-Boy • Cuban Sammy

SCAN FOR INFO

SOME BASICS

Reservations:	NO
Spirits:	FULL BAR
Parking:	LOT/STREET
Outdoor Dining:	YES

SPICE STATION

1438 Boulevard of the Arts
941-343-2894
spicestationsrq.com

DOWNTOWN	THAI/SUSHI	COST: $$

HOURS: Lunch: Mon-Sat, 11AM to 3PM
Dinner: Mon-Sat 4:30PM to 9PM • CLOSED SUNDAY

WHAT TO EXPECT: Casual Asian Cuisine • Quaint And Comfortable
Vegetarian Options • Thai And Sushi • Nice Outdoor Space

BEST BITES: Thai Calamari • Panang Beef • Ginger Pork
Grouper With Ginger • Amazing Chicken
Tom Yum Goong • Duck With Chili & Basil • Sushi

SOME BASICS

SCAN FOR MENU

Reservations:	YES
Spirits:	BEER/WINE
Parking:	LOT/STREET
Outdoor Dining:	YES

STAR THAI AND SUSHI

240 Avenida Madera*
941-217-6758
starthaisushisiestakey.com

SIESTA KEY	ASIAN	COST: $$

HOURS: Wed-Mon, 12PM to 11PM
CLOSED TUESDAY

WHAT TO EXPECT: Sushi • Siesta Village • Very Friendly Staff
Live Music • Great For A Date • Karaoke!

BEST BITES: Roasted Duck Noodle Soup • Sushi • Panang Curry
Crab Rangoon • Larb Gai • Tom Yum
Pad Thai • Soft Shell Crab • Three Buddies

SOME BASICS

SCAN FOR MENU

Reservations:	YES
Spirits:	FULL BAR
Parking:	STREET/LOT
Outdoor Dining:	YES

STATE STREET EATING HOUSE
1533 State Street
941-951-1533
statestreetsrq.com

DOWNTOWN	**AMERICAN**	**COST: $$**

HOURS: Tues-Fri, 5:30M to 11PM
Brunch: Sat & Sun, 10:30AM to 2:30PM

WHAT TO EXPECT: Great For A Date • Comfort Food • Good Wine List
Adult Lounge Scene • Excellent Cocktails

BEST BITES: Red Curry Mussels • Blistered Shishito Peppers
Pork Ragu • Prime Flat Iron Steak • Fried Chicken
State Street Burger • Hand Cut Garlic Parm Fries

SCAN FOR MENU

SOME BASICS
Reservations:	YES
Spirits:	FULL BAR
Parking:	STREET/GARAGE
Outdoor Dining:	YES

STOTTLEMYER'S SMOKEHOUSE
19 East Road
941-312-5969
stottlemyerssmokehouse.com

	BBQ	**COST: $$**

HOURS: Mon-Wed, 11:30AM to 8PM • Thur, 11:30AM to 9PM
Fri & Sat, 11:30PM to 10PM • Sun, 11:30AM to 9PM

WHAT TO EXPECT: Good For Families • Easy On The Wallet
Live Music • Casual Florida Dining Experience

BEST BITES: Fried Green Tomatoes • Smokehouse Salad
Beef Brisket • Famous Fried Chicken • Pulled Pork
Smoked Sausage Sandwich • Cuban Sandwich

SCAN FOR MENU

SOME BASICS
Reservations:	YES
Spirits:	FULL BAR
Parking:	LOT
Outdoor Dining:	YES

SARASOTA SUSHI
YOUR BEST ROLLS ROLL HERE!

Looking for sushi in Sarasota? You're going to have a decision to make. We have some fantastic and creative sushi chefs who call Sarasota their home. We've got 20+ places where you can indulge. Space is limited here, so we have personally curated a list of some of the best places in town (subject to debate, of course). Whether you're sitting at the bar or at a table with a group of friends, you can't go wrong with any of these places. Oh, just say "OMAKASE" and watch the magic happen...

DaRuMa Japanese Steak House • 5459 Fruitville Rd • 342-6600
WHAT TO EXPECT: Sushi + Teppan tableside cooking. This place is great for groups and big parties. Now open in The Landings.

Drunken Poet Café • 1572 Main St. • 955-8404
WHAT TO EXPECT: Sushi + Thai. A large selection of sushi. Downtown location. Also, lots of cooked options to choose from.

Jpan Restaurant • 3800 S. Tamiami Trl. • 954-5726
WHAT TO EXPECT: Always great. Never a miss here. BIG sushi menu. Super creative presentations. Also, across from UTC mall.

Kuro Sushi • 8126 Lakewood Ranch Main St. • 422-5876
WHAT TO EXPECT: Upscale sushi experience. Japanese whiskies. Try the Omakase Experience! New in the fall of 2025!

Pacific Rim • 1859 Hillview St. • 330-0218
WHAT TO EXPECT: One of Sarasota's most established sushi restaurants. Good for groups. Lots of cooked dishes too.

Samurai Japanese Fusion • 1936 Hillview St. • 777-7707
WHAT TO EXPECT: New (2024). Lots of creative and delicious sushi, sashimi, and rolls. They feature sake flights!

Star Thai & Sushi • 240 Avenida Madera • 217-6758
WHAT TO EXPECT: Really creative & well-presented sushi dishes. Lots of Thai choices as well. Friendly Siesta Key atmosphere.

SUMMER HOUSE STEAK & SEAFOOD

149 Avenida Messina
941-260-2675
summerhousesiestakey.com

SIESTA KEY	STEAKHOUSE	COST: $$$

HOURS: Sun-Thur, 4PM to 10PM
Fri & Sat, 4PM to 11PM

WHAT TO EXPECT: Always Busy • Upscale Dining • Fantastic Service
One Of Sarasota's Best Brunches • Excellent Wine List

BEST BITES: Colossal Shrimp Cocktail • Lobscargot
Lobster Bisque • 18oz Bone-In Rib Eye • Diver Scallops
16oz Pork Tomahawk • Pinot Noir Braised Short Rib

SCAN FOR MENU

SOME BASICS
Reservations:	YES
Spirits:	FULL BAR
Parking:	STREET/VALET
Outdoor Dining:	YES

SUNCOAST CAFÉ

400 Airport Avenue E.
941-484-0100
suncoastcafe.com

VENICE	CARIBBEAN	COST: $$

HOURS: Wed-Sun, 7:30AM to 2PM
CLOSED MONDAY & TUESDAY

WHAT TO EXPECT: Small, Cozy & Casual • At The Venice Airport
Say HI To Chef Tony! • Go Once And You'll Be A Regular

BEST BITES: Stuffed French Toast • St. Lucian Breakfast Quesadilla
Flight Crew's Omelet • Award Winning Chili • Reuben
Chicken Creole • Pilot's Choice Cuban • Burgers

SCAN FOR MENU

SOME BASICS
Reservations:	NO
Spirits:	NONE
Parking:	LOT
Outdoor Dining:	NO

SUNNYSIDE CAFÉ
4900 North Tamiami Trail
941-359-9500
sunnysidesrq.com

NORTH TRAIL	EUROPEAN	COST: $$$

HOURS: Tues-Fri, 9AM to 3PM • Sat & Sun, 8AM to 3PM
Wed-Sat, 5PM to 9PM

WHAT TO EXPECT: Hidden Gem • Great Breakfasts
Hungarian "Flavored" Menu

BEST BITES: Greek God Omelet • Avolicious Omelet
Eggs Benedict • Sunnyside Burger • Pork Chop Milanese
Hungarian Style Roasted Duck • Rack Of Lamb

SOME BASICS
SCAN FOR MENU

Reservations:	YES
Spirits:	BEER/WINE
Parking:	LOT
Outdoor Dining:	YES

SUN GARDEN CAFÉ
210 Avenida Madera
941-346-7170
sungardencafe.com

SIESTA KEY	AMERICAN	COST: $$

HOURS: Daily, 7:30AM to 1:30PM

WHAT TO EXPECT: Casual Island Lunch • Nice Outdoor Seating
Sandwich/Soup/Salad Combos

BEST BITES: Charleston Grits • Bikini Bagel • Garden Omelets
Shrimp Benedict • Adluh Mills Pancakes • Paninis
Curried Chicken Soup • Southern Fried Salad

SOME BASICS
SCAN FOR MENU

Reservations:	NO
Spirits:	BEER/WINE
Parking:	STREET
Outdoor Dining:	YES

TANDOOR

8453 Cooper Creek Boulevard
941-926-3077
tandoorsarasota.net

LAKEWOOD RANCH	INDIAN	COST: $$

HOURS: Lunch: Tue-Sun, 11:30PM to 2:30PM
Dinner: Tue-Sun, 5PM to 9PM • CLOSED MONDAY

WHAT TO EXPECT: Upscale Atmosphere • Serving Since 2001
Authentic Traditional Indian Cuisine • Lots Of Parking

BEST BITES: Aloo Tikki • Paneer Pakora • Tikka Masala
Madras Curry • Chicken Makhani • Channa Masala
Aloo Saag • Chicken Biryani • Chicken Tandoori

SCAN FOR MENU

SOME BASICS
Reservations:	YES
Spirits:	FULL BAR
Parking:	LOT
Outdoor Dining:	NO

TASTE OF HONG KONG

2224 Gulf Gate Drive
941-922-6765
tasteofhongkongsrq.com

GULF GATE	ASIAN	COST: $$

HOURS: Lunch: Tue-Sat, 11:30AM to 2:30PM
Dinner: Tues-Sat, 4PM to 9:30PM • Sun, 4:30PM to 9PM

WHAT TO EXPECT: Great For A Carry Out • Big Menu!
Good For Families • Lunch Specials

BEST BITES: Peking Delight • Roast Duck • Hunan Shrimp
Thai Basil Shrimp • Black Pepper Beef • Spicy XO Beef
Egg Drop Soup • Mei Fun & Lo Mein • Moo Goo Gai Pan

SCAN FOR MENU

SOME BASICS
Reservations:	NO
Spirits:	BEER/WINE
Parking:	LOT
Outdoor Dining:	NO

TAVERNA TOSCANA
1301 6th Avenue W.
941-357-7772
tavernatoscana.com

BRADENTON	ITALIAN	COST: $$$

HOURS: Daily, 4M to 10PM

WHAT TO EXPECT: Top Chef Fabio Viviani • Tuscan Dining Experience
Dry Aged Steaks! • Nice Outdoor Dining Space

BEST BITES: Fabio's Waygu Meatball • Seafood Cioppino
Osso Bucco • Wedge Salad • Tutta Carne Pizza
Shrimp Fra Diavolo • Crispy Brussel Sprouts

SOME BASICS
SCAN FOR MENU

Reservations:	YES
Spirits:	FULL BAR
Parking:	STREET/LOT
Outdoor Dining:	YES

TOASTED MANGO CAFÉ
1371 Boulevard of the Arts*
941-388-7728
toastedmangocafe.com

NORTH TRAIL	AMERICAN	COST: $$

HOURS: Daily, 7:30AM to 2:30PM

WHAT TO EXPECT: Good For Families • Casual Dining • Great Service
Lots Of Menu Choices • Busy On Weekends

BEST BITES: Avocado Toast • Eggs Benedict • Biscuits And Gravy
Waffle N' Egg • Egg Salad Sandwich • Cobb Salad
The Debbie Sandwich • Smoked Salmon Platter

SOME BASICS
SCAN FOR MENU

Reservations:	NO
Spirits:	BEER/WINE
Parking:	STREET
Outdoor Dining:	NO

TOASTED YOLK CAFÉ

3750 South Tamiami Trail
941-444-0049
thetoastedyolk.com/locations/downtown-sarasota/

SOUTH TRAIL	AMERICAN	COST: $$

HOURS: Daily, 7AM to 3PM

WHAT TO EXPECT: BIG Breakfasts • Counter Service
Good Lunch Time Meet Up Spot • Friendly Service

BEST BITES: Donuts "Churro Style" • Big Ben Omelet • Yolkwich
The Toasted Yolk! • California Club Sandwich
Salmon Salad • Soup & Sandwich Combo

SCAN FOR MENU

SOME BASICS

Reservations:	NO
Spirits:	NONE
Parking:	LOT
Outdoor Dining:	YES

TOMMY BAHAMA

465 John Ringling Boulevard
941-388-2888
tommybahama.com/restaurants-and-marlin-bars/locations/sarasota

ST ARMANDS	AMERICAN	COST: $$

HOURS: Mon-Thur, 11AM to 9:30PM • Fri, 11AM to 10PM
Sat, 10AM to 10PM • Sun, 10AM to 9:30PM

WHAT TO EXPECT: Great Happy Hour • Dine & Shop!
Upscale Casual Atmosphere • Nice Outdoor Dining Spaces

BEST BITES: World Famous Coconut Shrimp • Scallop Sliders
Lump Blue Crab Bisque • All-American Burger
Blackened Mahi Mahi Tacos • Bungalow Salad

SCAN FOR MENU

SOME BASICS

Reservations:	YES
Spirits:	FULL BAR
Parking:	STREET/GARAGE
Outdoor Dining:	YES

TONY'S CHICAGO BEEF

6569 Superior Avenue*
941-922-7979
tonyschicagobeef.com

GULF GATE	AMERICAN	COST: $

HOURS: Mon-Sat, 11AM to 9PM
CLOSED SUNDAY

WHAT TO EXPECT: Great For Lunch • Easy On The Wallet
Chicago Style Food • Counter And Table Seating

BEST BITES: Chicago Dog • Italian Beef Sandwich • Chicago Brat
Char-Grilled Burgers • Pork Chop Sandwich
Maxwell Street Polish Sausage • Pizza Puffs

SCAN FOR MENU

SOME BASICS

Reservations:	NO
Spirits:	BEER/WINE
Parking:	LOT/STREET
Outdoor Dining:	YES

TRATTORIA BELLA NAPOLI   **NEW**

1551 Main Street
941-330-9200
trattoriabellanapoli.com

DOWNTOWN	ITALIAN	COST: $$$

HOURS: Lunch & Dinner: Tues-Sun
CLOSED MONDAY

WHAT TO EXPECT: Neapolitan-Italian Cuisine • Upscale Atmosphere
Online Reservations • Main Street Location

BEST BITES: Zuppa Di Fagioli • Insalata Alle Pere
Antipasto Bella Napoli • Linguine Alle Vongole
Cotoletta Di Pollo • Pizza!

SCAN FOR MENU

SOME BASICS

Reservations:	YES
Spirits:	BEER/WINE
Parking:	STREET
Outdoor Dining:	YES

TRIPLETAIL SEAFOOD & SPIRITS

4870 South Tamiami Trail
941-529-0555
tripletailsrq.com

THE LANDINGS	SEAFOOD	COST: $$$

HOURS: Sun-Thur, 3PM to 9PM
Fri & Sat, 3PM to 10PM

WHAT TO EXPECT: Upscale, Casual Seafood • Happy Hour
Busy In Season • Handcrafted Cocktails

BEST BITES: Street Tacos • Lobster Mac & Cheese • Grouper Bites
Smoked Fish Dip • Fishcamp Chowder • Oysters
Tripletail • Crab Cakes • Ribeye Steak • Lobster Roll

SCAN FOR MENU

SOME BASICS

Reservations:	YES
Spirits:	FULL BAR
Parking:	LOT
Outdoor Dining:	YES

TURMERIC INDIAN BAR & GRILL

1001 Cocoanut Avenue
941-212-2622
turmericsarasota.com

ROSEMARY DIST	INDIAN	COST: $$$

HOURS: Mon, Wed, Thur, Sun, 11AM to 10PM
Fri & Sat, 11AM to 11PM • CLOSED TUESDAY

WHAT TO EXPECT: Indian "Fusion" Cuisine • Private Dining
Event Catering • Upscale Dining Atmosphere

BEST BITES: Dahi Aloo Puri • Lamb Boti Kebab • Momos
Chicken Tikka • Butter Chicken • Chana Masala
Dosa Stuffed • Biryani • Stuffed Naan

SCAN FOR MENU

SOME BASICS

Reservations:	YES
Spirits:	FULL BAR
Parking:	STREET
Outdoor Dining:	YES

TZEVA
1255 North Palm Avenue (Art Ovation Hotel)
941-316-0808
tzevasarasota.com

DOWNTOWN	MEDITERRANEAN	COST: $$

HOURS: Daily - Breakfast, Lunch, and Dinner

WHAT TO EXPECT: Modern Mediterranean Cuisine • Special Events
First Floor - Art Ovation Hotel • Good For Groups

BEST BITES: Shakshuka • Crab Benny • Greek Omelet
Israeli Salad • Lamb Loin Shashlik • Falafel
Toasted Feta Cheese • Black Sesame Brulée

SOME BASICS
SCAN FOR MENU

Reservations:	YES
Spirits:	FULL BAR
Parking:	GARAGE
Outdoor Dining:	YES

EXPERIENCE A SARASOTA FOOD TOUR

KEY CULINARY TOURS
WHAT TO EXPECT: Culinary walking tours of neighborhoods in
Sarasota, St. Armands, Anna Maria island and Venice. Lunch
and dinner tours. A great opportunity to sample local foods; meet
restaurateurs, discover Sarasota neighborhoods, and meet new
friends! They're Sarasota's original culinary touring company.
MORE INFO: keyculinarytours.com or 941-893-4664

SUNSET FOOD TOURS
WHAT TO EXPECT: The Sunset Sip and Dine Tour is a great way
to see Downtown Sarasota and eat your way through it. They
also offer a Taste of Downtown Food Tour. For something a little
different, try the Sarasota Street Food Tour.
MORE INFO & BOOK ONLINE AT: sunsetfoodtours.com/srq

VALENTINO'S PIZZERIA
4045 Clark Road
941-921-9600
valentinopizzeria.com

EXPO ON CLARK	ITALIAN	COST: $$

HOURS: Mon-Sat, 11AM to 9PM
CLOSED SUNDAY

WHAT TO EXPECT: "Jersey Style" Italian Food • Great Pizza
Good For Groups • Good For Families • Delivery Available

BEST BITES: Jersey Platter • Buratte Caprese • Toni Salad
Stracciatella • Escarole & Bean Soup • Franky Marsala
Flo's Ravioli • Pizza! • Limoncello Marscapone

SCAN FOR MENU

SOME BASICS

Reservations:	YES
Spirits:	BEER/WINE
Parking:	LOT
Outdoor Dining:	NO

VERNONA
711 Manatee Avenue E.
941-284-0416
vernonagourmet.com

BRADENTON	HUNGARIAN	COST: $$

HOURS: Mon-Sat, 7:30AM to 9PM (Closed from 2:30 to 5:30)
Sunday, 7:30PM to 2:30PM

WHAT TO EXPECT: Authentic Hungarian Cuisine • Catering Available
Special Events • Bradenton Riverwalk

BEST BITES: Hortobagyi Palacsinta • Chicken Paprikas
Rantott Sajt • Chicken Schnitzel • Rákóczi Túrós
Meatloaf Hadik Style • Csülkös Strapacska

SCAN FOR MENU

SOME BASICS

Reservations:	YES
Spirits:	BEER/WINE
Parking:	STREET
Outdoor Dining:	NO

VILLAGE CAFÉ

5133 Ocean Boulevard
941-349-2822
villagecafeonsiesta.com

SIESTA KEY	AMERICAN	COST: $$

HOURS: Daily, 7:30AM to 2PM

WHAT TO EXPECT: Family Owned • Dog Friendly Outdoor Dining
Casual Dining • Open Since 1995 • Local SK Favorite!

BEST BITES: Belgian Waffles • Cinnamon Roll French Toast
The Works Omelet • Avocado Toast • Lox & Bagel
Burgers • Tom's Greek Salad • Daily Specials

SOME BASICS

SCAN FOR MENU

Reservations:	NO
Spirits:	BEER/WINE
Parking:	STREET
Outdoor Dining:	YES

VERONICA FISH & OYSTER

1830 South Osprey Avenue
941-366-1342
veronicafishandoyster.com

SOUTHSIDE VILLAGE	SEAFOOD	COST: $$$

HOURS: Mon-Thur, 5PM to 9PM • Fri & Sat, 5PM to 10PM
CLOSED SUNDAY

WHAT TO EXPECT: Busy, Lively Dining Room • Handmade Cocktails
Raw Bar • Upscale Dining • Happy Hour

BEST BITES: Grilled Octopus • Bibb Salad • Smoked Fish Dip
Lobster Fra Diavolo • Pork Belly • Fresh Catch
Thai Crispy Whole Snapper • Blackened Mahi BLT

SOME BASICS

SCAN FOR MENU

Reservations:	YES
Spirits:	FULL BAR
Parking:	LOT/STREET
Outdoor Dining:	YES

VINO VINO

2063 Siesta Drive
941-354-0234
vinovinorestaurant.com

SOUTHGATE	ITALIAN	COST: $$

HOURS: Mon-Sat, 5PM to 10PM

WHAT TO EXPECT: Local Favorite • Southern Italian Cuisine
Intimate Atmosphere • Homemade Desserts

BEST BITES: Friselle Baresi • Calamari Guazzetto
Calamari Guazzetto • Porkchop Picatta
Troccoli Allo Scoglio • Tiramisu

SCAN FOR MENU

SOME BASICS
Reservations:	YES
Spirits:	BEER/WINE
Parking:	LOT/STREET
Outdoor Dining:	NO

ABOUT US

Way back in April 2002, we started dineSarasota as a way to bring up-to-date restaurant and dining information to Sarasota locals and visitors. Our annual printed dining guides and our website, dineSarasota.com, have grown right along with the ever-expanding Sarasota dining scene. Whether you're just visiting or you're a native, we're here to help you make the most of your local dining experiences.

WALT'S FISH MARKET AND RESTAURANT
4144 South Tamiami Trail
941-921-4605
waltsfishmarketrestaurant.com

SOUTH TRAIL	SEAFOOD	COST: $$

HOURS: Mon-Thur, 11AM to 9PM • Sun, 11AM to 10PM
Market, 9AM to 8PM

WHAT TO EXPECT: Restaurant & Market • Live Music • Casual Dining
Busy In Season • Since 1918!

BEST BITES: Stone Crab (In Season) • Smoked Fish Spread
Peel & Eat Shrimp • Lobster Bisque • Oysters
Fresh Fish Daily • Off The Hook Oscar • Grouper Bowl

SOME BASICS
SCAN FOR MENU

Reservations:	NO
Spirits:	FULL BAR
Parking:	LOT
Outdoor Dining:	YES

WOLFIE'S RASCAL HOUSE
1420 Boulevard of the Arts
941-312-4072
originalwolfies.com

ROSEMARY DIST	DELI	COST: $$

HOURS: Daily, 11AM to Last Call

WHAT TO EXPECT: NY Style Deli • Yes, The Same Wolfie's As Miami
Bustling Atmosphere • Happy Hour • Grab & Go Carry Out

BEST BITES: Smoked Fish • Fresh NY Bagels • Matzo Ball Soup
Broasted Chicken • Brisket • Knish • Reuben Sandwich
Corned Beef & Pastrami Sandwiches • Sol's NY Cheesecake

SOME BASICS
SCAN FOR MENU

Reservations:	NO
Spirits:	FULL BAR
Parking:	STREET
Outdoor Dining:	YES

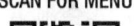

LOCAL FARMERS MARKET INFORMATION

SARASOTA FARMERS MARKET
Lemon Avenue
Downtown Sarasota
Saturdays (Year Round)
7AM to 1PM
Rain or Shine
70+ Vendors
sarasotafarmersmarket.org

DOWNTOWN BRADENTON PUBLIC MARKET
Old Main Street (12 St. W)
Saturdays (October thru May)
9AM to 2PM
realizebradenton.com/about-the-market

SIESTA KEY FARMERS MARKET
5211 Ocean Boulevard
Sundays (Year Round)
8AM to 12PM
Rain or Shine
siestakeyfarmersmarket.org

PHILLIPPI FARMHOUSE MARKET
Phillippi Estates Park (5500 South Tamiami Trail)
Wednesdays (October thru April)
9AM to 2PM
50+ Vendors
farmhousemarket.org

VENICE FARMERS MARKET
Venice City Hall (401 West Venice Avenue)
Saturdays (Year Round)
8AM to 12PM
thevenicefarmersmarket.org

WHAT'S IN SEASON?

Our Sarasota area farmer's markets really give locals and visitors a taste of fresh Florida flavor. But, our markets are more than a place just to stock up for the week. They're a place to mingle with friends, enjoy some music, or catch up on the latest neighborhood news!

Now you have a good list of places to buy the freshest locally grown produce. But, what's the best time of year to enjoy Florida's fruits and vegetables? When are they at their peak of freshness? Here's a little help.

WINTER > Bell Pepper • Eggplant • Grapefruit Strawberries • Squash • Tomatoes • Arugula • Kale
SPRING > Cantaloupe • Guava • Lettuce • Mushrooms Oranges • Papaya • Radish • Swiss Chard • Strawberries
SUMMER > Avocado • Guava • Mango • Eggplant Peanuts • Sweet Corn • Watermelon • Snow Peas
FALL > Cucumber • Grapefruit • Mushrooms • Lettuce Snap Beans • Tangerines • Tomatoes • Peppers

We have super fresh seafood here in Sarasota. You can usually find a plentiful supply of grouper, red snapper, pompano, and mahi at our farmer's markets. Of course, you can always find fresh Gulf shrimp in a variety of sizes.

The most anticipated seafood season runs from October 15th through May 1st. That's stone crab season! You're best off grabbing these tasty delights towards the beginning of season when they're the most plentiful.

WOODEN ROOSTER

1564 Main Steet
941-953-7111
thewoodenrooster.com

DOWNTOWN	AMERICAN	COST: $$

HOURS: Mon-Thur, 11AM to 4PM
Fri & Sat, 9AM to 4PM

WHAT TO EXPECT: Breakfast & Lunch • Super Casual
Organic Produce • Good Downtown Lunch Spot

BEST BITES: Crepes, Lots Of Them! • Vegan Tartine Duo
Smoked Salmon Salad • Ice Cream
Espresso • Daily Seasonal Soups

SCAN FOR MENU

SOME BASICS

Reservations:	NO
Spirits:	BEER/WINE
Parking:	STREET
Outdoor Dining:	NO

WORD OF MOUTH

6604 Gateway Avenue
941-925-2400
originalwordofmouth.com

GULF GATE	AMERICAN	COST: $$

HOURS: Daily, 8AM to 2PM

WHAT TO EXPECT: Daily Specials • Casual Dining
Good For Families • Counter Seating Available

BEST BITES: Fresh Baked Muffins • Smoothie Of The Day
Omelets • Frittatas • Eggs Benedict
Curried Egg Salad Sandwich • Classic BLT • Cobb Salad

SCAN FOR MENU

SOME BASICS

Reservations:	NO
Spirits:	BEER/WINE
Parking:	LOT/STREET
Outdoor Dining:	NO

YODER'S RESTAURANT
3434 Bahia Vista Street
941-955-7771
yodersrestaurant.com

PINECRAFT	AMISH	COST: $

HOURS: Mon-Sat, 7AM to 8PM
CLOSED SUNDAY

WHAT TO EXPECT: Great For Families • Easy On The Wallet
Busy In Season • Fantastic Service • Pie!!

BEST BITES: Daily Lunch, Dinner & Soup Specials • Great Sides!
Turkey Manhattan • Yoder's Famous Fried Chicken
Roast Turkey • Traditional BLT • Mom's Meatloaf

SOME BASICS
Reservations: NO
Spirits: NONE
Parking: LOT
Outdoor Dining: NO

SCAN FOR MENU

YOKOSO RAMEN
3422 Clark Road
941-265-1600
yokosoramen.com

	ASIAN	COST: $$

HOURS: Lunch & Dinner, Wed-Mon
CLOSED TUESDAY

WHAT TO EXPECT: REAL Ramen • Good For Families
Milk Teas • Lots Of Parking

BEST BITES: Gyoza • Shrimp Shumai • Yokoso Steamed Buns
Ramen Menu - Tonkotsu, Curry, Shoyu, Nabeyaki

SOME BASICS
Reservations: NO
Spirits: NONE
Parking: LOT
Outdoor Dining: NO

SCAN FOR MENU

Restaurant Name	Address	Phone #
Alma de España	1830 S Osprey Ave	365-8426
Alpine Steakhouse	4520 S Tamiami Trl	922-3797
Amore	180 N Lime Ave	383-1111
Andrea's	2085 Siesta Dr	951-9200
Anna Maria Oyster Bar	6696 Cortez Rd	792-0077
Anna Maria Oyster Bar	1525 51st Ave E	721-7773
Anna's Deli	6535 Midnight Pass	348-4888
Apollonia Grill	8235 Cooper Creek	359-4816
Arts & Central	611 Central Ave	306-2356
Athens Family Rest.	2300 Bee Ridge Rd	706-4121
Atria Bread + Coffee	4120 LWR Blvd	751-1016
Bangkok Restaurant	4791 Swift Rd	922-0703
Baker & Wife	2157 Siesta Dr	960-1765
Bar Hana	1289 N Palm Ave	536-9717
The Barnyard	620 MLK Ave W	896-8760
Beach House Restaurant	200 Gulf Dr N	779-2222
Bean Coffeehouse	5138 Ocean Blvd	260-6400
Bella Vita Italian Kitchen	105 N Beneva Rd	365-5555
Beso	30 S Lemon Ave	279-2999
Big Water Fish Market	6641 Midnight Pass	554-8101
Blu Kuzina	25 N Blvd of Pres.	388-2619
Blue Dolphin Café	470 John Ringling Bl	388-3566
BLVD Café	1580 Blvd of the Arts	203-8102
Boca Sarasota	21 S Lemon Ave	256-3565
The Breakfast Company	7246 55th Ave E	201-6002
The Breakfast House	1817 Fruitville Rd	366-6860
Brick's Smoked Meats	1528 State St	993-1435

Restaurant Name	Address	Phone #
Brine Seafood	2250 Gulf Gate Dr	404-5639
Bulgogi House	1472 Main St	559-5678
Bushido Izayaki	3688 Webber St	217-5635
Café Barbosso	5501 Palmer Crossing	922-7999
Café Epicure	1298 Main St	366-5648
Café Gabbiano	5104 Ocean Blvd	349-1423
Café on St. Armands	431 St Armands Cir	388-4415
Capo Pazzo	2053 Reynolds St	487-8677
Capt. Curt's Oyster Bar	1200 Old Stickney Pt	349-3885
Casa Masa	2773 Bee Ridge Rd.	922-8226
Casey Key Fish House	801 Blackburn Pt Rd	966-1901
Cask & Ale	1548 Main St	702-8740
C'est La Vie!	1553 Main St	906-9575
Chateau 13	535 13th St W	226-0110
Chaz 51 Steakhouse	549 US-41 BYP	484-6200
Circo	1435 2nd St	253-0978
Clasico Italian Chophse	1342 Main St	203-5115
The Columbia	411 St Armands Cir	388-3987
Comida	1534 State St	324-5985
Connors Steakhouse	3501 S Tamiami Trl	260-3232
Corkscrew Deli	4982 S Tamiami Trl	925-3955
The Cottage	153 Avenida Messina	312-9300
Crab & Fin	420 St Armands Cir	388-3964
Cuba 1958	1766 Main St	280-1958
The Daiquiri Deck	5250 Ocean Blvd	349-8697
Darrell's	215 S Tamiami Trl	485-9900

Restaurant Name	Address	Phone #
DaRuMa Japanese	5459 Fruitville Rd	342-6600
DaRuMa Japanese	4910 S Tamiami Trl	552-9465
D'Corato Ristorante	322 S Washington Blvd	330-1300
Deep Lagoon Seafood	482 Blackburn Pt Rd	770-3337
Der Dutchman	3713 Bahia Vista	955-8007
Dim Sum King	8194 Tourist Center Dr	306-5848
Divan Turkish Cuisine	6525 Superior Ave	924-3030
Double Deez Hot Dogs	3009 Gulf Dr N	251-5595
Doughboy Swift	2881 Clark Rd	315-7011
Drift Kitchen	700 Benjamin Franklin	388-2161
Drunken Poet Café	1572 Main St	955-8404
Dry Dock Waterfront	412 Gulf of Mexico Dr	383-0102
Duo Döner & Deli	5049 Ocean Blvd	298-9660
Dutch Valley	6721 S Tamiami Trl	924-1770
Duval's, Fresh, Local...	1435 Main St	312-4001
1818 Grill	1818 S Osprey Ave	955-1818
83 Tavern	8383 S Tamiami Trl	203-5312
El Toro Bravo	3218 Clark Rd	924-0006
Element	1413 Main St	724-8585
EnRich Bistro	5239 Manatee Ave W	289-1299
Euphemia Haye	5540 Gulf of Mexico Dr	383-3633
15 South by Napule	15 S Blvd of Pres	867-8081
1592 Wood Fired Kitch	1592 Main St	365-2234
The Fat Rabbit	1359 Main St	780-1151
Figaro Bistro	1944 Hillview St	960-2109
Fins At Sharky's	1600 Harbor Dr S	999-3467
Flavio's on Siesta	5239 Ocean Blvd	349-0995

Restaurant Name	Address	Phone #
Florence & Spice Boys	4990 S Tamiami Trl	405-3890
Flower Child	6532 University Pkwy	373-0199
Focaccia Sandwiches	2300 Bee Ridge Rd	924-2268
Food + Beer	6528 Superior Ave	952-3361
Fork & Hen	1990 Main St	444-7094
Fresta's Italian American	6392 Lockwood Ridge	203-8467
Fuego Comida & Tequila	11615 St Rd 70	751-5252
Gecko's Grill & Pub	6606 S Tamiami Trl	248-2020
Gecko's Grill & Pub	5588 Palmer Crossing	923-6061
Gecko's Grill & Pub	351 N Cattlemen Rd	378-0077
Gecko's Grill & Pub	1900 Hillview St	953-2929
The Grasshopper	7253 S Tamiami Trl	923-3688
Graze Street AMI	3218 E Bay Dr	896-6320
The Green Orchid	1534 Mound St	265-8194
GROVE Restaurant	10670 Boardwalk Lp	893-4321
Harry's Continental Kit.	525 St Judes Dr	383-0777
Hive Bar	2881 Clark Rd	888-0382
The Hub Baha Grill	5148 Ocean Blvd	349-6800
Ichiban Sushi	2724 Stickney Pt Rd	924-1611
Indigenous	239 Links Ave	706-4740
Inkawasi Peruvian	10667 Boardwalk Lp	360-1110
Island House Tap & Grl.	5110 Ocean Blvd	312-9205
Jack Dusty	1111 Ritz-Carlton Dr	309-2266
Jersey Girl Bagels	5275 University Pkwy	388-8910
Joey D's Chicago Style	3811 Kenny Dr.	378-8900
Jpan Sushi & Grill	3800 S Tamiami Trl	954-5726
Jpan Sushi & Grill	229 N Cattlemen Rd	954-5726
JR's Old Packinghouse	987 S Packinghse Rd	371-9358

Restaurant Name	Address	Phone #
Kacey's Seafood	4904 Fruitville Rd	378-3644
Kojo	1289 N Palm Ave	536-9717
Kolukan	6644 Gateway Ave	921-3133
Kore Steakhouse	1561 Lakefront Dr	928-5673
La Norma	5370 Gulf of Mex Dr	383-6262
La Violetta	4837 Swift Rd	927-8716
Lazy Lobster	5350 Gulf of Mex Dr	388-0440
Lefty's Oyster Bar	428 N Lemon Ave	954-8688
Lenny'z Pizza & Bar	6645 Midnight Pass	378-3644
Libby's Bistro	1917 S Osprey Ave	487-7300
Lila	1576 Main St	296-1042
Lo' Key Island Grill	5620 Gulf of Mexico	387-0089
The Lobster Pot	5157 Ocean Blvd	349-2323
L'Opera Bakery & Bistro	2336 Gulf Gate Dr	922-2253
Lovely Square	6559 Gateway Ave	724-2512
Lucky 8	1812 S Osprey Ave	779-5299
The Mable	2831 N Tamiami Trl	487-7373
Mad Moe's	106 N Tamiami Trl, Os	966-9700
Mademoiselle Paris	8527 Cooper Creek Bl	355-2323
Mademoiselle Paris	1605 Main St	544-4021
Madfish Grill	4059 Cattlemen Rd	377-3474
Main Bar Sandwich Shp	1944 Main St	955-8733
Maison Blanche	2605 Gulf of Mex	383-8088
Malmosto	2085 Siesta Dr	706-1460
Mar-Vista Restaurant	760 Broadway St	383-2391
Marcello's Ristorante	4155 S Tamiami Trl	921-6794
Marina Jack's	2 Marina Plaza	365-4243

Restaurant Name	Address	Phone #
Mattison's City Grille	1 N Lemon Ave	330-0440
Mattison's Forty One	7275 S Tamiami Trl	921-3400
Mean Dean's	6059 26th St W	251-5435
Mediterraneo	1970 Main St	365-4122
Michael's On East	1212 East Ave	366-0007
Michelle's Brown Bag	630 S Orange Ave	365-5858
Miguel's	6631 Midnight Pass	349-4024
Millie's Café	3900 Clark Rd	923-4054
Mirna's Cuban Cuisine	2901 N Tamiami Trl	316-9793
Molly's Pub	1562 Main St	366-7711
Monk's Steamer Bar	6690 Superior Ave	927-3388
Mouthole Smashburgers	2637 Mall Dr	746-4653
My Village Pub (MVP)	5200 Ocean Blvd	777-6787
99 Bottles Taproom	1445 2nd St	487-7874
Naked Farmer	215 N Cattlemen Rd	870-9412
Namo Izakaya	1439 Main St	362-3332
Napule Ristorante	7129 S Tamiami Trl	556-9639
New Pass Grill	1505 Ken Thompson	388-3050
131 Main	6608 University Pkwy	394-0131
Oasis Café	3542 S Osprey Ave	957-1214
The Old Salty Dog	5023 Ocean Blvd	349-0158
The Old Salty Dog	160 Ken Thompson	388-4311
O'Leary's Tiki Bar	5 Bayfront Dr	203-4771
Ophelia's on the Bay	9105 Midnight Pass	349-2212
Origin Beer & Pizza	3837 Hillview St	316-9222
Origin Beer & Pizza	5070 Clark Rd	217-6533
Osteria 500	1580 Lakefront Dr	866-8962

Restaurant Name	Address	Phone #
Ortygia	1418 13th St W	741-8646
Owen's Fish Camp	516 Burns Ct	951-6936
Owen's Fish Camp	6516 University Pkwy	951-5052
Trattoria Bella Napoli	1551 Main St	330-9200
Pacific Rim	1859 Hillview St	330-8071
Palm Avenue Deli	1297 N Palm Ave	263-3742
Parrot Patio Bar & Grill	3602 Webber St	952-3352
Pastry Art Bakery	1512 Main St	955-7545
Patrick's 1481	1481 Main St	955-1481
Pazzo on Orange	481 N Orange Ave	364-4682
Phillippi Creek Oyster	5363 S Tamiami Trl	925-4444
Pho Cali	1578 Main St	955-2683
Pi 3.14 Craft Beer	5263 Ocean Blvd	346-1188
Piccolo Italian Market	6518 Gateway Ave	923-2202
Pie on Main	1507 Main St	217-6370
Pier 22	1200 1st Avenue W	748-8087
Pigfish	5377 Mcintosh Rd	777-5220
Pop's Sunset Grill	112 Circuit Rd	488-3177
Pork Roll Pete's	4657 Cortez Rd	896-3333
Post Kitchen + Bar	8433 Cooper Ck Blvd	259-4850
Prime Serious Steak	133 S Tamiami Trl	837-8325
Red Plum Asian Bistro	7119 S Tamiami Trl	554-8816
Rendez-Vous Bakery	5336 Clark Rd	924-1234
Rendez-Vous Bakery	2117 Siesta Dr	552-9240
Rick's French Bistro	2177 Siesta Dr	957-0533
Ringside	233 Ben Franklin Dr	413-5992

Restaurant Name	Address	Phone #
Riverhouse Reef & Grill	995 Riverside Dr	729-0616
Rose & Ivy	1296 1st St	343-2122
Rosebud's Steakhouse	2215 S Tamiami Trl	918-8771
Rosemary & Thyme	511 N Orange Ave	955-7600
Sage	1216 1st St	445-5660
Samba Brazilian Stk	6115 S Tamiami Trl	586-2040
Samurai Japanese	1936 Hillview St	777-7707
Sandbar Spirits-Seafood	100 Spring Ave	778-0444
Schnitzel Kitchen	6521 Superior Ave	922-9299
Selva Grill	1345 Main St	362-4427
Serving Spoon	1825 S Osprey Ave	388-7235
Shakespeare's Eng. Pub	3550 S Osprey Ave	364-5938
Shaner's Pizza	6500 Superior	927-2708
Sharky's on the Pier	1600 Harbor Dr S	488-1456
Shebeen Irish Pub	6641 Midnight Pass	952-3070
Shore Diner	800 Broadway St	259-4600
Siegfried's Restaurant	1869 Fruitville Rd	330-9330
Siesta Key Oyster Bar	5238 Ocean Blvd	346-5443
Simon's Coffee House	5900 S Tamiami Trl	926-7151
Southside Deli	1825 Hillview St	330-9302
Speaks Clam Bar	29 N Blvd of Pres.	232-7633
Spearfish Grille	1265 Old Stickney Pt	349-1970
Spice Station	1438 Blvd of the Arts	343-2894
Star Thai & Sushi	240 Avenida Madera	217-6758
State St. Eating House	1533 State St	951-1533
Stottlemeyer's Smokehs	19 East Rd	312-5969
The Summer House	149 Avenida Messina	206-2675

Restaurant Name	Address	Phone #
Suncoast Café	400 Airport Ave E	484-0100
Sunnyside Café	4900 N Tamiami Trl	359-9500
Sun Garden Café	210 Avenida Madera	346-7170
Tandoor	8453 Cooper Creek	926-3070
Taste of Hong Kong	2224 Gulf Gate Dr	922-6765
Taverna Toscana	1301 6th Ave W	357-7772
Toasted Mango Café	1371 Blvd of the Arts	388-7728
Toasted Mango Café	6621 Midnight Pass	552-6485
Toasted Yolk Café	3750 S Tamiami Trl	444-0049
Tommy Bahama's	465 John Ringling Blvd	388-2888
Tony's Chicago Beef	6569 Superior Ave	922-7979
Trattoria Bella Napoli	1551 Main St	330-9200
Tripletail Seafood	4870 S Tamiami Trl	529-0555
Turmeric	1001 Cocoanut Ave	212-2622
Tzeva	1255 N Palm Ave	413-7425
Valentino's Pizza	4045 Clark Rd	921-9600
Vernona	711 Manatee Ave E	284-0416
Veronica Fish & Oyster	1830 S Osprey Ave	366-1342
Village Café	5133 Ocean Blvd	349-2822
Vino Vino	2063 Siesta Dr	354-0234
Walt's Fish Market	4144 S Tamiami Trl	921-4605
Wolfie's Rascal House	1454 Blvd of the Arts	312-4072
Wooden Rooster	1564 Main St	953-7111
Word of Mouth	6604 Gateway Ave	925-2400
Yoder's Restaurant	3434 Bahia Vista	955-7771
Yokoso Ramen	3422 Clark Rd	265-1600

AMERICAN		
Restaurant Name	**Address**	**Phone #**
Arts & Central	611 Central Ave	306-2356
Atria Bread + Coffee	4120 LWR Blvd	751-1016
Baker & Wife	2157 Siesta Dr	960-1765
The Barnyard	620 MLK Ave W	896-8760
Bijou Café	1287 First St	366-8111
Blue Dolphin Café	470 John Ringling Bl	388-3566
BLVD Café	1580 Blvd of the Arts	203-8102
Boca Sarasota	21 S. Lemon Ave	256-3565
The Breakfast Company	7246 55th Ave E	201-6002
The Breakfast House	1817 Fruitville Rd	366-6860
Brick's Smoked Meats	1528 State St	993-1435
Clayton's Siesta Grille	1256 Old Stickney Pt	349-2800
The Cottage	153 Avenida Messina	312-9300
Daiquiri Deck Raw Bar	5250 Ocean Blvd	349-8697
Daiquiri Deck Raw Bar	325 John Ringling Blvd	388-3325
Daiquiri Deck Raw Bar	300 W Venice Ave	488-0649
Daiquiri Deck Raw Bar	1250 Stickney Pt Rd	312-2422
Darrell's	215 S Tamiami Trl	485-9900
Double Deez Hot Dogs	3009 Gulf Dr N	251-5595
Drift Kitchen	700 Benjamin Franklin	388-2161
Der Dutchman	3713 Bahia Vista	955-8007
Dutch Valley Restaurant	6731 S Tamiami Trl	924-1770
Duval's, Fresh, Local...	1435 Main St	312-4001
1818 Grill	1818 S Osprey Ave	955-1818

AMERICAN		
Restaurant Name	Address	Phone #
83 Tavern	8383 S Tamiami Trl	203-5312
EnRich Bistro	5239 Manatee Ave W	289-1299
Euphemia Haye	5540 Gulf of Mexico Dr	383-3633
The Fat Rabbit	1359 Main St	780-1151
Flower Child	6532 University Pkwy	373-0199
Food + Beer	6528 Superior Ave	952-3361
Fork & Hen	1990 Main St	444-7094
Gecko's Grill & Pub	6606 S Tamiami Trl	248-2020
Gecko's Grill & Pub	1900 Hillview St	953-2929
Gecko's Grill & Pub	5588 Palmer Crossing	923-6061
Gecko's Grill & Pub	351 N Cattlemen Rd	378-0077
Gilligan's Island Bar	5253 Ocean Blvd	349-4759
Graze Street AMI	3218 E Bay Dr	896-6320
The Green Orchid	1534 Mound St	265-8194
GROVE Restaurant	10670 Boardwalk Lp	893-4321
Harry's Continental Kit.	525 St Judes Dr	383-0777
Hive Bar	2881 Clark Rd	888-0382
The Hub Baha Grill	5148 Ocean Blvd	349-6800
Indigenous	239 Links Ave	706-4740
Island House Tap & Grl.	5110 Ocean Blvd	312-9205
Jack Dusty	1111 Ritz-Carlton Dr	309-2266
Joey D's Chicago Style	3811 Kenny Dr.	378-8900
JR's Old Packinghouse	987 S Packinghouse	371-9358
Libby's	1917 S Osprey Ave	487-7300
Lo' Key Island Grill	5620 Gulf of Mexico	387-0089

AMERICAN		
Restaurant Name	Address	Phone #
Lovely Square	6559 Gateway Ave	724-2512
Lucky 8	1812 S Osprey Ave	779-5299
The Mable	2831 N Tamiami Trl	487-7373
Mad Moe's	106 N Tamiami Trl, Os	966-9700
Madfish Grill	4059 Cattlemen Rd	377-3474
Marina Jack's	2 Marina Plaza	365-4243
Mattison's City Grille	1 N Lemon Ave	330-0440
Mattison's Forty One	7275 S Tamiami Trl	921-3400
Mean Deans	6059 26th St W	251-5435
Michael's On East	1212 East Ave	366-0007
Millie's Café	3900 Clark Rd	923-4054
Mouthole Smashburgers	2637 Mall Dr	746-4653
Munchies 420 Café	6639 Superior Ave	929-9893
My Village Pub (MVP)	5200 Ocean Blvd	777-6787
99 Bottles Taproom	1445 2nd St	487-7874
New Pass Grill	1505 Ken Thompson	388-3050
131 Main	6608 University Pkwy	394-0131
Oasis Café	3542 S Osprey Ave	957-1214
The Old Salty Dog	5023 Ocean Blvd	349-0158
The Old Salty Dog	160 Ken Thompson Pk	388-4311
The Old Salty Dog	1485 S Tamiami Trl	483-1000
O'Leary's Tiki Bar	5 Bayfront Dr	953-7505
Ophelia's on the Bay	9105 Midnight Pass	349-2212
Parrot Patio Bar & Grill	3602 Webber St	952-3352
Pastry Art Bakery	1512 Main St	955-7545

AMERICAN		
Restaurant Name	Address	Phone #
Patrick's 1481	1481 Main St	955-1481
Pier 22	1200 1st Avenue W	748-8087
Pop's Sunset Grill	112 Circuit Rd	488-3177
Post Kitchen + Bar	8433 Cooper Ck Blvd	259-4850
Ringside	233 Ben Franklin Dr	413-5992
Rosemary & Thyme	511 N Orange Ave	955-7600
Sage	1216 1st St	445-5660
The Sandbar	100 Spring Ave	778-0444
Serving Spoon	1825 S Osprey Ave	388-7235
Sharky's on the Pier	1600 Harbor Dr S	488-1456
Shore Diner	800 Broadway St	259-4600
Siesta Key Oyster Bar	5238 Ocean Blvd	346-5443
Simon's Coffee House	5900 S Tamiami Trl	926-7151
State St. Eating House	1533 State St	951-1533
Stottlemeyer's Smokehs	19 East Rd	312-5969
Sun Garden Café	210 Avenida Madera	346-7170
Toasted Mango Café	6621 Midnight Pass	552-6485
Toasted Mango Café	1371 Blvd of the Arts	388-7728
Toasted Yolk Café	3750 S Tamiami Trl	444-0049
Tommy Bahama's	465 John Ringling Blvd	388-2888
Tony's Chicago Beef	6569 Superior Ave	922-7979
Village Café	5133 Ocean Blvd	349-2822
Wooden Rooster	1564 Main St	953-7111
Word of Mouth	6604 Gateway Ave	925-2400
Yoder's Restaurant	3434 Bahia Vista	955-7771

ASIAN		
Restaurant Name	Address	Phone #
Bar Hana	1289 N Palm Ave	536-9717
Blue Koi	3801 Macintosh Rd	388-7738
DaRuMa Japanese	4910 S Tamiami Trl	552-9465
Dim Sum King	8194 Tourist Center Dr	306-5848
Drunken Poet Café	1572 Main St	955-8404
Jpan Sushi & Grill	3800 S Tamiami Trl	954-5726
Jpan Sushi & Grill	229 N Cattlemen Rd	954-5726
Kojo	1289 N Palm Ave	536-9717
Kore Steakhouse	1561 Lakefront Dr	928-5673
Namo Izakaya	1439 Main St	362-3332
Pacific Rim	1859 Hillview St	330-8071
Pho Cali	1578 Main St	955-2683
Red Plum Asian Bistro	7119 S Tamiami Trl	554-8816
Rose & Ivy	1296 1st St	343-2122
Samurai Japanese	1936 Hillview St	777-7707
Spice Station	1438 Blvd of the Arts	343-2894
Star Thai & Sushi	240 Avenida Madera	217-6758
Yokoso Ramen	3422 Clark Rd	265-1600

CUBAN, MEXICAN, SPANISH, AND LATIN		
Alma de España	1830 S Osprey Ave	365-8426
Beso	30 S Lemon Ave	279-2999
Bohemios Tapas Bar	3246 Clark Rd	260-9784
Casa Masa	2773 Bee Ridge Rd.	922-8226
Comida	1534 State St	324-5985

CUBAN, MEXICAN, SPANISH, AND LATIN		
Restaurant Name	Address	Phone #
Circo	1435 2nd St	253-0978
The Columbia	411 St Armands Cir	388-3987
Cuba 1958	1766 Main St	280-1958
El Toro Bravo	2720 Stickney Pt Rd	924-0006
The Grasshopper	7253 S Tamiami Trl	923-3688
Kolukan	6644 Gateway Ave	921-3133
Mirna's Cuban Cuisine	2901 N Tamiami Trl	316-9793
Samba Brazilian Stk	6115 S Tamiami Trl	586-2040

DELI		
Anna's Deli	6535 Midnight Pass	348-4888
Corkscrew Deli	4982 S Tamiami Trl	925-3955
Focaccia Sandwiches	2300 Bee Ridge Rd	924-2268
Jersey Girl Bagels	5275 University Pkwy	388-8910
Main Bar Sandwich Shp	1944 Main St	955-8733
Michelle's Brown Bag	1819 Main St	365-5858
Palm Avenue Deli	1297 N Palm Ave	263-3742
Piccolo Italian Market	6518 Gateway Ave	923-2202
Pork Roll Pete's	4657 Cortez Rd	896-3333
Southside Deli	1825 Hillview St	330-9302
Wolfie's Rascal House	1454 Blvd of the Arts	312-4072

ENGLISH, IRISH & SCOTTISH		
Molly's Pub	1562 Main St	366-7711
Shakespeare's	3550 S Osprey Ave	364-5938
Shebeen Irish Pub	6641 Midnight Pass	952-3070

FRENCH		
Restaurant Name	Address	Phone #
C'est La Vie!	1553 Main St	906-9575
Figaro Bistro	1944 Hillview St	960-2109
L'Opera Bakery & Bistro	2336 Gulf Gate Dr	922-2253
Mademoiselle Paris	8527 Cooper Creek Bl	355-2323
Maison Blanche	2605 Gulf of Mexico Dr	383-8088
Miguel's	6631 Midnight Pass	349-4024
Rick's French Bistro	2177 Siesta Dr	957-0533
GREEK		
Apollonia Grill	8235 Cooper Creek	359-4816
Athens Family Rest.	2300 Bee Ridge Rd	706-4121
1592 Wood Fired Kitch	1592 Main St	365-2234
INDIAN		
Tandoor	8453 Cooper Creek	926-3070
Turmeric	1001 Cocoanut Ave	212-2622
ITALIAN		
Amore	180 N Lime Ave	383-1111
Andrea's	2085 Siesta Dr	951-9200
Bella Vita Italian Kitchen	105 N Beneva Rd	365-5555
Café Barbosso	5501 Palmer Crossing	922-7999
Café Epicure	1298 Main St	366-5648
Café Gabbiano	5104 Ocean Blvd	349-1423
Capo Pazzo	2053 Reynolds St	487-8677

ITALIAN		
Restaurant Name	**Address**	**Phone #**
Flavio's on Siesta	5239 Ocean Blvd	349-0995
Fresta's Italian American	6392 Lockwood Ridge	203-8467
15 South by Napule	15 S Blvd of Pres	867-8081
La Norma	5370 Gulf of Mex Dr	383-6262
La Violetta	4837 Swift Rd	927-8716
Malmosto	2085 Siesta Dr	706-1460
Marcello's Ristorante	4155 S Tamiami Trl	921-6794
Mediterraneo	1970 Main St	365-4122
Napule Ristorante	7129 S Tamiami Trl	556-9639
Osteria 500	1580 Lakefront Dr	866-8962
Pazzo on Orange	481 N Orange Ave	364-4682
Piccolo Italian Market	6518 Gateway Ave	923-2202
Taverna Toscana	1301 6th Ave W	357-7772
Trattoria Bella Napoli	1551 Main St	330-9200
Valentino's Pizza	4045 Clark Rd	921-9600
Vino Vino	2063 Siesta Dr	354-0234

SEAFOOD		
Anna Maria Oyster Bar	6696 Cortez Rd	792-0077
Big Water Fish Market	6641 Midnight Pass	554-8101
Brine Seafood	2250 Gulf Gate Dr	404-5639
Capt. Curt's Oyster Bar	1200 Old Stickney Pt	349-3885
Casey Key Fish House	801 Blackburn Pt Rd	966-1901
Crab & Fin	420 St Armands Cir	388-3964
Dry Dock Waterfront	412 Gulf of Mexico Dr	383-0102

SEAFOOD		
Restaurant Name	Address	Phone #
Deep Lagoon Seafood	482 Blackburn Pt Rd	770-3337
Duval's, Fresh, Local...	1435 Main St	312-4001
Fins At Sharky's	1600 Harbor Dr S	999-3467
Kacey's Seafood	4904 Fruitville Rd	378-3644
Lazy Lobster	5350 Gulf of Mexico Dr	388-0440
Lefty's Oyster Bar	428 N Lemon Ave	954-8688
The Lobster Pot	5157 Ocean Blvd	349-2323
Mar-Vista Restaurant	760 Broadway St	383-2391
Monk's Steamer Bar	6690 Superior Ave	927-3388
Ophelia's on the Bay	9105 Midnight Pass	349-2212
Owen's Fish Camp	516 Burns Ct	951-6936
Phillippi Creek Oyster	5363 S Tamiami Trl	925-4444
Pigfish	5377 Mcintosh Rd	777-5220
Siesta Key Oyster Bar	5238 Ocean Blvd	346-5443
Speaks Clam Bar	29 N Blvd of Pres.	232-7633
Spearfish Grille	1265 Old Stickney Pt	349-1970
Tripletail Seafood	4870 S Tamiami Trl	529-0555
Veronica Fish & Oyster	1830 S Osprey Ave	366-1342
Walt's Fish Market	4144 S Tamiami Trl	921-4605

STEAKHOUSE		
Alpine Steakhouse	4520 S Tamiami Trl	922-3797
Chaz 51 Steakhouse	549 US-41 BYP	484-6200
Connors Steakhouse	3501 S Tamiami Trl	260-3232
Prime Serious Steak	133 S Tamiami Trl	837-8325
Rosebud's Steakhouse	2215 S Tamiami Trl	918-8771
The Summer House	149 Avenida Messina	206-2675

ANNA MARIA AND BRADENTON		
Restaurant Name	Address	Phone #
Atria Bread + Coffee	4120 LWR Blvd	751-1016
The Barnyard	620 MLK Ave W	896-8760
The Breakfast Company	7246 55th Ave E	201-6002
Double Deez Hot Dogs	3009 Gulf Dr N	251-5595
EnRich Bistro	5239 Manatee Ave W	289-1299
Graze Street AMI	3218 E Bay Dr	896-6320
Lo' Key Island Grill	5620 Gulf of Mexico	387-0089
Pier 22	1200 1st Avenue W	748-8087
Pork Roll Pete's	4657 Cortez Rd	896-3333
The Sandbar	100 Spring Ave	778-0444
Taverna Toscana	1301 6th Ave W	357-7772
Vernona	711 Manatee Ave E	284-0416

DOWNTOWN		
Amore	180 N Lime Ave	383-1111
Bar Hana	1289 N Palm Ave	536-9717
Beso	30 S Lemon Ave	279-2999
Bavaro's Pizza	27 Fletcher Ave	552-9131
Bijou Café	1287 First St	366-8111
BLVD Café	1580 Blvd of the Arts	203-8102
Boca Sarasota	21 S Lemon Ave	256-3565
The Breakfast House	1817 Fruitville Rd	366-6860
Brick's Smoked Meats	1528 State St	993-1435
Café Epicure	1298 Main St	366-5648
C'est La Vie!	1553 Main St	906-9575
Circo	1435 2nd St	253-0978

DOWNTOWN		
Restaurant Name	**Address**	**Phone #**
Clasico Italian Chophse	1341 Main St	957-0700
Comida	1534 State St	324-5985
Cuba 1958	1766 Main St	280-1958
Drunken Poet Café	1572 Main St	955-8404
Duval's, Fresh, Local...	1435 Main St	312-4001
1592 Wood Fired Kitch	1592 Main St	365-2234
The Fat Rabbit	1359 Main St	780-1151
Fork & Hen	1990 Main St	444-7094
Il Panificio	1703 Main St	366-5570
Indigenous	239 Links Ave	706-4740
Jack Dusty	1111 Ritz-Carlton Dr	309-2266
Kojo	1289 N Palm Ave	536-9717
Lefty's Oyster Bar	428 N Lemon Ave	954-8688
Lila	1576 Main St	296-1042
Main Bar Sandwich Shp	1944 Main St	955-8733
Marina Jack's	2 Marina Plaza	365-4243
Mattison's City Grille	1 N Lemon Ave	330-0440
Mediterraneo	1970 Main St	365-4122
Michelle's Brown Bag	630 S Orange Ave	365-5858
Molly's Pub	1562 Main St	366-7711
99 Bottles Taproom	1445 2nd St	487-7874
Namo Izakaya	1439 Main St	362-3332
Owen's Fish Camp	516 Burns Ct	951-6936
Palm Avenue Deli	1297 N Palm Ave	263-3742
Pastry Art Bakery	1512 Main St	955-7545

DOWNTOWN		
Restaurant Name	**Address**	**Phone #**
Patrick's 1481	1481 Main St	955-1481
Pazzo on Orange	481 N Orange Ave	364-4682
Pho Cali	1578 Main St	955-2683
Pie on Main	1507 Main St	217-6370
Rose & Ivy	1296 1st St	343-2122
Rosemary & Thyme	511 N Orange Ave	955-7600
Sage	1216 1st St	445-5660
Selva Grill	1345 Main St	362-4427
Siegfried's Restaurant	1869 Fruitville Rd	330-9330
Spice Station	1438 Blvd of the Arts	343-2894
State St Eating House	1533 State St	951-1533
Trattoria Bella Napoli	1551 Main St	330-9200
Turmeric	1001 Cocoanut Ave	212-2622
Tzeva	1255 N Palm Ave	413-7425
Wolfie's Rascal House	1454 Blvd of the Arts	312-4072
Wooden Rooster	1564 Main St	953-7111
GULF GATE		
Brine Seafood	2250 Gulf Gate Dr	404-5639
Divan Turkish Cuisine	6525 Superior Ave	924-3030
Dolce Italia	6606 Superior Ave	921-7007
Food + Beer	6528 Superior Ave	952-3361
Kolukan	6644 Gateway Ave	921-3133
L'Opera Bakery & Bistro	2336 Gulf Gate Dr	922-2253
Lovely Square	6559 Gateway Ave	724-2512

GULF GATE

Restaurant Name	Address	Phone #
Monk's Steamer Bar	6690 Superior Ave	927-3388
Mouthole Smashburgers	2637 Mall Dr	746-4653
Piccolo Italian Market	6518 Gateway Ave	923-2202
Schnitzel Kitchen	6521 Superior Ave	922-9299
Shaner's Pizza	6500 Superior	927-2708
Tony's Chicago Beef	6569 Superior Ave	922-7979
Word of Mouth	6604 Gateway Ave	925-2400

LONGBOAT KEY & LIDO KEY

Drift Kitchen	700 Benjamin Franklin	388-2161
Dry Dock Waterfront	412 Gulf of Mexico Dr	383-0102
Euphemia Haye	5540 Gulf of Mexico Dr	383-3633
Lazy Lobster	5350 Gulf of Mexico Dr	388-0440
Harry's Continental Kit.	525 St Judes Dr	383-0777
Maison Blanche	2605 Gulf of Mexico Dr	383-8088
Mar-Vista Restaurant	760 Broadway St	383-2391
New Pass Grill	1505 Ken Thompson	388-3050
Ringside	233 Ben Franklin Dr	413-5992
Shore Diner	800 Broadway St	259-4600

LAKEWOOD RANCH & UNIVERSITY PARK

Apollonia Grill	8235 Cooper Creek	359-4816
Dim Sum King	8194 Tourist Center Dr	306-5848
Flower Child	6532 University Pkwy	373-0199

LAKEWOOD RANCH & UNIVERSITY PARK

Restaurant Name	Address	Phone #
GROVE Restaurant	10670 Boardwalk Lp	893-4321
Inkawasi Peruvian	10667 Boardwalk Lp	360-1110
Jpan Sushi & Grill	229 N Cattlemen Rd	954-5726
Jersey Girl Bagels	5275 University Pkwy	388-8910
Naked Farmer	215 N Cattlemen Rd	870-9412
Mademoiselle Paris	8527 Cooper Creek Bl	355-2323
131 Main	6608 University Pkwy	394-0131
Post Kitchen + Bar	8433 Cooper Ck Blvd	259-4850
Tandoor	8453 Cooper Creek	926-3070

NORTH TAMIAMI TRAIL

The Mable	2831 N Tamiami Trl	487-7373
Mirna's Cuban Cuisine	2901 N Tamiami Trl	316-9793
Sunnyside Café	4900 N Tamiami Trl	359-9500

ST. ARMANDS KEY

Café on St. Armands	431 St Armands Cir	388-4415
The Columbia	411 St Armands Cir	388-3987
Crab & Fin	420 St Armands Cir	388-3964
Blue Dolphin Café	470 John Ringling Bl	388-3566
15 South by Napule	15 S Blvd of Pres	867-8081
Speaks Clam Bar	29 N Blvd of Pres	232-7633
Tommy Bahama's	465 John Ringling Blvd	388-2888

SIESTA KEY		
Restaurant Name	Address	Phone #
Anna's Deli	6535 Midnight Pass	348-4888
Bean Coffeehouse	5138 Ocean Blvd	260-6400
Big Water Fish Market	6641 Midnight Pass	554-8101
Café Gabbiano	5104 Ocean Blvd	349-1423
Capt. Curt's Oyster Bar	1200 Old Stickney Pt	349-3885
The Cottage	153 Avenida Messina	312-9300
Daiquiri Deck Raw Bar	5250 Ocean Blvd	349-8697
Duo Döner & Deli	5049 Ocean Blvd	298-9660
Flavio's on Siesta	5239 Ocean Blvd	349-0995
The Hub Baha Grill	5148 Ocean Blvd	349-6800
Island House Tap & Grl.	5110 Ocean Blvd	312-9205
Lenny'z Pizza & Bar	6645 Midnight Pass	378-3644
The Lobster Pot	5157 Ocean Blvd	349-2323
Miguel's	6631 Midnight Pass	349-4024
My Village Pub (MVP)	5200 Ocean Blvd	777-6787
The Old Salty Dog	5023 Ocean Blvd	349-0158
Ophelia's on the Bay	9105 Midnight Pass	349-2212
Siesta Key Oyster Bar	5238 Ocean Blvd	346-5443
Shebeen Irish Pub	6641 Midnight Pass	952-3070
Spearfish Grille	1265 Old Stickney Pt	349-1970
Star Thai & Sushi	240 Avenida Madera	217-6758
The Summer House	149 Avenida Messina	206-2675
Sun Garden Café	210 Avenida Madera	346-7170
Toasted Mango Café	6621 Midnight Pass	552-6485
Village Café	5133 Ocean Blvd	349-2822

SOUTH TAMIAMI TRAIL		
Restaurant Name	Address	Phone #
Alpine Steakhouse	4520 S Tamiami Trl	922-3797
Capo Pazzo	2053 Reynolds St	487-8677
Connors Steakhouse	3501 S Tamiami Trl	260-3232
Corkscrew Deli	4982 S Tamiami Trl	925-3955
DaRuMa Japanese	4910 S Tamiami Trl	552-9465
Demetrio's Pizzeria	4410 S Tamiami Trl	922-1585
Dutch Valley Rest.	6731 S Tamiami Trl	924-1770
83 Tavern	8383 S Tamiami Trl	203-5312
Florence & Spice Boys	4990 S Tamiami Trl	405-3890
Gecko's Grill & Pub	4870 S Tamiami Trl	923-8896
Marcello's Ristorante	4155 S Tamiami Trl	921-6794
Mattison's Forty One	7275 S Tamiami Trl	921-3400
Michael's On East	1212 East Ave	366-0007
Napule Ristorante	7129 S Tamiami Trl	556-9639
Phillippi Creek Oyster	5363 S Tamiami Trl	925-4444
Red Plum Asian Bistro	7119 S Tamiami Trl	554-8816
Samba Brazilian Stk	6115 S Tamiami Trl	586-2040
Simon's Coffee House	5900 S Tamiami Trl	926-7151
Tripletail Seafood	4870 S Tamiami Trl	529-0555
Toasted Yolk Café	3750 S Tamiami Trl	444-0049
Walt's Fish Market	4144 S Tamiami Trl	921-4605

Join the other 18,000+
Follow us on Facebook!

dineSarasota

18K followers • 588 following

SOUTHSIDE VILLAGE		
Restaurant Name	Address	Phone #
Alma de España	1830 S Osprey Ave	365-8426
1818 Grill	1818 S Osprey Ave	955-1818
Figaro Bistro	1944 Hillview St	960-2109
Libby's Brasserie	1917 S Osprey Ave	487-7300
Lucky 8	1812 S Osprey Ave	779-5299
Origin Beer & Pizza	3837 Hillview St	316-9222
Pacific Rim	1859 Hillview St	330-8071
Samurai Japanese	1936 Hillview St	777-7707
Veronica Fish & Oyster	1830 S Osprey Ave	366-1342

SOUTHGATE		
Andrea's	2085 Siesta Dr	951-9200
Baker & Wife	2157 Siesta Dr	960-1765
Connors Steakhouse	3501 S Tamiami Trl	260-3232
Fleming's Steakhouse	2001 Siesta Dr	358-9463
Malmosto	2085 Siesta Dr	706-1460
Rick's French Bistro	2177 Siesta Dr	957-0533
Vino Vino	2063 Siesta Dr	354-0234

UNIVERSITY TOWN CENTER (UTC)		
Brio Tuscan Grille	190 Univ Town Ctr Dr	702-9102
The Capital Grille	180 Univ Town Ctr Dr	256-3647
Cheesecake Factory	130 Univ Town Ctr Dr	256-3760
Seasons 52	170 Univ Town Ctr Dr	702-9652
Sophies	120 Univ Town Ctr Dr	444-3077

LIVE MUSIC		
Restaurant Name	Address	Phone #
Capt. Curt's Oyster Bar	1200 Old Stickney Pt	349-3885
Casey Key Fish House	801 Blackburn Pt Rd	966-1901
Gecko's Grill & Pub	4870 S Tamiami Trl	923-8896
The Hub Baha Grill	5148 Ocean Blvd	349-6800
JR's Old Packinghouse	987 S Packinghouse	371-9358
Marina Jack's	2 Marina Plaza	365-4243
Mattison's City Grille	1 N Lemon Ave	330-0440
Mattison's Forty One	7275 S Tamiami Trl	921-3400
Parrot Patio Bar & Grill	3602 Webber St	952-3352
Pop's Sunset Grill	112 Circuit Rd	488-3177
Sharky's on the Pier	1600 Harbor Dr S	488-1456
Siesta Key Oyster Bar	5238 Ocean Blvd	346-5443
Star Thai & Sushi	240 Avenida Madera	217-6758
Stottlemeyer's Smokehs	19 East Rd	312-5969
Walt's Fish Market	4144 S Tamiami Trl	921-4605

CATERING		
Brick's Smoked Meats	1528 State St	993-1435
Daiquiri Deck Raw Bar	5250 Ocean Blvd	349-8697
Gecko's Grill & Pub	4870 S Tamiami Trl	923-8896
Harry's Continental Kit.	525 St Judes Dr	383-0777

We've Got Your Sarasota Restaurant News!

SUBSCRIBE TODAY

sarasota bites

CATERING		
Restaurant Name	**Address**	**Phone #**
JR's Old Packinghouse	987 S Packinghouse	371-9358
Mattison's Forty One	7275 S Tamiami Trl	921-3400
Michael's On East	1212 East Ave	366-0007
Village Café	5133 Ocean Blvd	349-2822

EASY ON YOUR WALLET		
Athens Family Rest.	2300 Bee Ridge Rd	706-4121
Atria Bread + Coffee	4120 LWR Blvd	751-1016
Anna's Deli	6535 Midnight Pass	348-4888
The Barnyard	620 MLK Ave W	896-8760
Bean Coffeehouse	5138 Ocean Blvd	260-6400
The Breakfast House	1817 Fruitville Rd	366-6860
Casa Masa	2773 Bee Ridge Rd.	922-8226
Casey Key Fish House	801 Blackburn Pt Rd	966-1901
Circo	1435 2nd St	253-0978
Corkscrew Deli	4982 S Tamiami Trl	925-3955
Double Deez Hot Dogs	3009 Gulf Dr N	251-5595
Dim Sum King	8194 Tourist Center Dr	306-5848
Dutch Valley Rest.	6731 S Tamiami Trl	924-1770
Flower Child	6532 University Pkwy	373-0199
Focaccia Sandwiches	2300 Bee Ridge Rd	924-2268
Joey D's Chicago Style	3811 Kenny Dr.	378-8900
Il Panificio	1703 Main St	366-5570
Jersey Girl Bagels	5275 University Pkwy	388-8910
Lo' Key Island Grill	5620 Gulf of Mexico	387-0089
Lovely Square	6559 Gateway Ave	724-2512

EASY ON YOUR WALLET

Restaurant Name	Address	Phone #
The Mable	2831 N Tamiami Trl	487-7373
Main Bar Sandwich Shp	1944 Main St	955-8733
Michelle's Brown Bag	630 S Orange Ave	365-5858
Mouthole Smashburgers	2637 Mall Dr	746-4653
New Pass Grill	1505 Ken Thompson	388-3050
Pastry Art Bakery	1512 Main St	955-7545
Pho Cali	1578 Main St	955-2683
Piccolo Italian Market	6518 Gateway Ave	923-2202
Pork Roll Pete's	4657 Cortez Rd	896-3333
Tony's Chicago Beef	6569 Superior Ave	922-7979
Yoder's Restaurant	3434 Bahia Vista	955-7771
Yokoso Ramen	3422 Clark Rd	265-1600
Wooden Rooster	1564 Main St	953-7111

BREAKFAST & LUNCH

Anna's Deli	6535 Midnight Pass	348-4888
Atria Bread + Coffee	4120 LWR Blvd	751-1016
Bean Coffeehouse	5138 Ocean Blvd	260-6400
Blue Dolphin Café	470 John Ringling Bl	388-3566
BLVD Café	1580 Blvd of the Arts	203-8102
The Breakfast Company	7246 55th Ave E	201-6002
The Breakfast House	1817 Fruitville Rd	366-6860
Lovely Square	6559 Gateway Ave	724-2512
Main Bar Sandwich Shp	1944 Main St	955-8733
Michelle's Brown Bag	630 S Orange Ave	365-5858
Millie's Café	3900 Clark Rd	923-4054
Oasis Café	3542 S Osprey Ave	957-1214

BREAKFAST & LUNCH		
Restaurant Name	Address	Phone #
Pastry Art Bakery	1512 Main St	955-7545
Sun Garden Café	210 Avenida Madera	346-7170
Suncoast Café	400 Airport Ave E	484-0100
Toasted Mango Café	6621 Midnight Pass	552-6485
Toasted Yolk Café	3750 S Tamiami Trl	444-0049
Village Café	5133 Ocean Blvd	349-2822
Word of Mouth	6604 Gateway Ave	925-2400
NEW		
Alma de España	1830 S Osprey Ave	365-8426
Bella Vita Italian Kitchen	105 N Beneva Rd	365-5555
Café on St. Armands	431 St Armands Cir	388-4415
Comida	1534 State St	324-5985
Doughboy Swift	2881 Clark Rd	315-7011
83 Tavern	8383 S Tamiami Trl	203-5312
Flower Child	6532 University Pkwy	373-0199
Fresta's Italian American	6392 Lockwood Ridge	203-8467
Lefty's Oyster Bar	428 N Lemon Ave	954-8688
Lo' Key Island Grill	5620 Gulf of Mexico	387-0089
Lucky 8	1812 S Osprey Ave	779-5299
Mirna's Cuban Cuisine	2901 N Tamiami Trl	316-9793
131 Main	6608 University Pkwy	394-0131
Pork Roll Pete's	4657 Cortez Rd	896-3333
Ringside	233 Ben Franklin Dr	413-5992
Samba Brazilian Stk	6115 S Tamiami Trl	586-2040
Tommy Bahama's	465 John Ringling Blvd	388-2888
Trattoria Bella Napoli	1551 Main St	330-9200

SPORTS + FOOD + FUN		
Restaurant Name	Address	Phone #
Capt. Curt's Oyster Bar	1200 Old Stickney Pt	349-3885
Daiquiri Deck Raw Bar	5250 Ocean Blvd	349-8697
Gecko's Grill & Pub	6606 S Tamiami Trl	248-2020
Gecko's Grill & Pub	1900 Hillview St	953-2929
Gecko's Grill & Pub	5588 Palmer Crossing	923-6061
The Old Salty Dog	5023 Ocean Blvd	349-0158
Mad Moe's	106 N Tamiami Trl, Os	966-9700
My Village Pub (MVP)	5200 Ocean Blvd	777-6787
Parrot Patio Bar & Grill	3602 Webber St	952-3352
Patrick's 1481	1481 Main St	955-1481
Pie on Main	1507 Main St	217-6370
Siesta Key Oyster Bar	5238 Ocean Blvd	346-5443

SUSHI		
Star Thai & Sushi	240 Avenida Madera	217-6758
DaRuMa Japanese	5459 Fruitville Rd	342-6600
DaRuMa Japanese	4910 S Tamiami Trl	552-9465
Drunken Poet Café	1572 Main St	955-8404
Jpan Sushi & Grill	3800 S Tamiami Trl	954-5726
Jpan Sushi & Grill	229 N Cattlemen Rd	954-5726
Ichiban Sushi	2724 Stickney Pt Rd	924-1611
Kojo	1289 N Palm Ave	536-9717
Pacific Rim	1859 Hillview St	330-8071
Red Plum Asian Bistro	7119 S Tamiami Trl	554-8816
Rose & Ivy	1296 1st St	343-2122
Samurai Japanese	1936 Hillview St	777-7707
Spice Station	1438 Blvd of the Arts	343-2894

GREAT BURGERS		
Restaurant Name	Address	Phone #
Alpine Steakhouse	4520 S Tamiami Trl	922-3797
The Barnyard	620 MLK Ave W	896-8760
Connors Steakhouse	3501 S Tamiami Trl	260-3232
Gecko's Grill & Pub	4870 S Tamiami Trl	923-8896
Gecko's Grill & Pub	1900 Hillview St	953-2929
Gecko's Grill & Pub	5588 Palmer Crossing	923-6061
Gecko's Grill & Pub	351 N Cattlemen Rd	378-0077
Hive Bar	2881 Clark Rd	888-0382
Food + Beer	6528 Superior Ave	952-3361
Indigenous	239 Links Ave	706-4740
Island House Tap & Grl.	5110 Ocean Blvd	312-9205
JR's Old Packinghouse	987 S Packinghouse	371-9358
Libby's Brasserie	1917 S Osprey Ave	487-7300
The Mable	2831 N Tamiami Trl	487-7373
Mouthole Smashburgers	2637 Mall Dr	746-4653
My Village Pub (MVP)	5200 Ocean Blvd	777-6787
New Pass Grill	1505 Ken Thompson	388-3050
Parrot Patio Bar & Grill	3602 Webber St	952-3352
Patrick's 1481	1481 Main St	955-1481
Pop's Sunset Grill	112 Circuit Rd	488-3177
Shakespeare's	3550 S Osprey Ave	364-5938
Siesta Key Oyster Bar	5238 Ocean Blvd	346-5443
Sunnyside Café	4900 N Tamiami Trl	359-9500
Tony's Chicago Beef	6569 Superior Ave	922-7979

NICE WINE LIST		
Restaurant Name	Address	Phone #
Amore	180 N Lime Ave	383-1111
Andrea's	2085 Siesta Dr	951-9200
Arts & Central	611 Central Ave	306-2356
Baker & Wife	2157 Siesta Dr	960-1765
Café Barbosso	5501 Palmer Crossing	922-7999
Café Gabbiano	5104 Ocean Blvd	349-1423
Café L'Europe	431 St Armands Cir	388-4415
Chaz 51 Steakhouse	549 US-41 BYP	484-6200
Connors Steakhouse	3501 S Tamiami Trl	260-3232
Duval's, Fresh, Local...	1435 Main St	312-4001
Euphemia Haye	5540 Gulf of Mexico Dr	383-3633
Figaro Bistro	1944 Hillview St	960-2109
Fins At Sharky's	1600 Harbor Dr S	999-3467
Flavio's on Siesta	5239 Ocean Blvd	349-0995
The Green Orchid	1534 Mound St	265-8194
GROVE Restaurant	10670 Boardwalk Lp	893-4321
Harry's Continental Kit.	525 St Judes Dr	383-0777
Hive Bar	2881 Clark Rd	888-0382
Indigenous	239 Links Ave	706-4740
Jack Dusty	1111 Ritz-Carlton Dr	309-2266
Maison Blanche	2605 Gulf of Mexico Dr	383-8088
Mattison's Forty One	7275 S Tamiami Trl	921-3400
Michael's On East	1212 East Ave	366-0007
Miguel's	6631 Midnight Pass	349-4024
Napule Ristorante	7129 S Tamiami Trl	556-9639

NICE WINE LIST		
Restaurant Name	Address	Phone #
Ophelia's on the Bay	9105 Midnight Pass	349-2212
Pier 22	1200 1st Avenue W	748-8087
Ringside	233 Ben Franklin Dr	413-5992
Rose & Ivy	1296 1st St	343-2122
Rosebud's Steakhouse	2215 S Tamiami Trl	918-8771
Rosemary & Thyme	511 N Orange Ave	955-7600
Sage	1216 1st St	445-5660
State St Eating House	1533 State St	951-1533
The Summer House	149 Avenida Messina	206-2675
Selva Grill	1345 Main St	362-4427
Tzeva	1255 N Palm Ave	413-7425
Veronica Fish & Oyster	1830 S Osprey Ave	366-1342

HELP MAKE A DIFFERENCE IN OUR SARASOTA-MANATEE COMMUNITY

Listed below are two local organizations that are striving to assist those in need in our Sarasota area. They could use your help. Please consider a donation to either (or both) this year.

ALL FAITHS FOOD BANK
WHAT THEY NEED: Donations of non-perishable, frozen, and perishable food items needed. Monetary donations are also accepted and can be made directly through their website.
MORE INFO: allfaithsfoodbank.org

MAYOR'S FEED THE HUNGRY PROGRAM
WHAT THEY NEED: Donations of food, time, and money are needed. This program hosts a large food drive in the month of November. Check their website for details or to make a monetary donation.
MORE INFO: mayorsfeedthehungry.org

A BEAUTIFUL WATER VIEW		
Restaurant Name	**Address**	**Phone #**
Casey Key Fish House	801 Blackburn Pt Rd	966-1901
Deep Lagoon Seafood	482 Blackburn Pt Rd	770-3337
Drift Kitchen	700 Benjamin Franklin	388-2161
Dry Dock Waterfront	412 Gulf of Mexico Dr	383-0102
Fins At Sharky's	1600 Harbor Dr S	999-3467
Jack Dusty	1111 Ritz-Carlton Dr	309-2266
Mar-Vista Restaurant	760 Broadway St	383-2391
Marina Jack's	2 Marina Plaza	365-4243
New Pass Grill	1505 Ken Thompson	388-3050
The Old Salty Dog	160 Ken Thompson Pk	388-4311
The Old Salty Dog	1485 S Tamiami Trl	483-1000
O'Leary's Tiki Bar	5 Bayfront Dr	953-7505
Ophelia's on the Bay	9105 Midnight Pass	349-2212
Phillippi Creek Oyster	5363 S Tamiami Trl	925-4444
Pier 22	1200 1st Avenue W	748-8087
Pop's Sunset Grill	112 Circuit Rd	488-3177
The Sandbar	100 Spring Ave	778-0444
Sharky's on the Pier	1600 Harbor Dr S	488-1456
Shore Diner	800 Broadway St	259-4600

LATER NIGHT MENU		
Bar Hana	1289 N Palm Ave	536-9717
Café Epicure	1298 Main St	366-5648
Capt. Curt's Oyster Bar	1200 Old Stickney Pt	349-3885

LATER NIGHT MENU		
Restaurant Name	Address	Phone #
Casey Key Fish House	801 Blackburn Pt Rd	966-1901
Circo	1435 2nd St	253-0978
The Cottage	153 Avenida Messina	312-9300
Daiquiri Deck Raw Bar	5250 Ocean Blvd	349-8697
Drunken Poet Café	1572 Main St	955-8404
Food + Beer	6528 Superior Ave	952-3361
Gecko's Grill & Pub	6606 S Tamiami Trl	248-2020
The Hub Baha Grill	5148 Ocean Blvd	349-6800
Island House Tap & Grl.	5110 Ocean Blvd	312-9205
JR's Old Packinghouse	987 S Packinghouse	371-9358
Lenny'z Pizza & Bar	6645 Midnight Pass	378-3644
The Mable	2831 N Tamiami Trl	487-7373
Mad Moe's	106 N Tamiami Trl, Os	966-9700
Mattison's City Grille	1 N Lemon Ave	330-0440
Monk's Steamer Bar	6690 Superior Ave	927-3388
My Village Pub (MVP)	5200 Ocean Blvd	777-6787
Origin Beer & Pizza	3837 Hillview St	316-9222
Palm Avenue Deli	1297 N Palm Ave	263-3742
Patrick's 1481	1481 Main St	955-1481
Shaner's Pizza	6500 Superior	927-2708
Sharky's on the Pier	1600 Harbor Dr S	488-1456
Siesta Key Oyster Bar	5238 Ocean Blvd	346-5443
Walt's Fish Market	4144 S Tamiami Trl	921-4605
Wolfie's Rascal House	1454 Blvd of the Arts	312-4072

SARASOTA FINE & FINER DINING

Restaurant Name	Address	Phone #
Andrea's	2085 Siesta Dr	951-9200
Bijou Café	1287 First St	366-8111
The Crow's Nest	1968 Tarpon Ctr Dr	484-9551
Euphemia Haye	5540 Gulf of Mexico Dr	383-3633
Indigenous	239 Links Ave	706-4740
Jack Dusty	1111 Ritz-Carlton Dr	309-2266
Maison Blanche	2605 Gulf of Mexico Dr	383-8088
Michael's On East	1212 East Ave	366-0007
Ophelia's on the Bay	9105 Midnight Pass	349-2212
Pier 22	1200 1st Avenue W	748-8087
Sage	1216 1st St	445-5660
The Summer House	149 Avenida Messina	206-2675

PIZZA PIE!

Baker & Wife	2157 Siesta Dr	960-1765
Bavaro's Pizza	27 Fletcher Ave	552-9131
Café Barbosso	5501 Palmer Crossing	922-7999
Café Epicure	1298 Main St	366-5648
Capo Pazzo	2053 Reynolds St	487-8677
Doughboy Swift	2881 Clark Rd	315-7011
83 Tavern	8383 S Tamiami Trl	203-5312
1592 Wood Fired Kitch	1592 Main St	365-2234
Flavio's Siesta Key	5239 Ocean Blvd	349-0995

PIZZA PIE!		
Restaurant Name	Address	Phone #
Joey D's Chicago Style	3811 Kenny Dr.	378-8900
Lenny'z Pizza & Bar	6645 Midnight Pass	378-3644
Malmosto	2085 Siesta Dr	706-1460
Mattison's City Grille	1 N Lemon Ave	330-0440
Mediterraneo	1970 Main St	365-4122
Napule Ristorante	7129 S Tamiami Trl	556-9639
Origin Beer & Pizza	3837 Hillview St	316-9222
Pazzo on Orange	481 N Orange Ave	364-4682
Pie on Main	1507 Main St	217-6370
Shaner's Pizza	6500 Superior	927-2708
Vacci Pizza & Cucina	4406 53rd Ave E	405-4131

UPSCALE CHAIN DINING		
Bonefish Grill	3971 S Tamiami Trl	924-9090
Bravo Coastal Kitchen	3501 S Tamiami Trl	316-0868
Brio Tuscan Grille	190 Univ Town Ctr Dr	702-9102
The Chart House	201 Gulf of Mex Dr	383-5593
California Pizza Kitchen	192 N Cattlemen Rd	203-6966
The Capital Grille	180 Univ Town Ctr Dr	256-3647
Cooper's Hawk	3130 Fruitville Comm	263-8100
CW Prime	1601 Gulf of Mex Dr	328-2000
Fleming's Steakhouse	2001 Siesta Dr	358-9463
Hyde Park Steakhouse	35 S Lemon Ave	366-7788
Ocean Prime	501 Quay Commons	404-1024
P.F. Chang's	766 S Osprey Ave	296-6002
Ruth's Chris Steakhouse	6700 S Tamiaml Trl	924-9442
Seasons 52	170 Univ Town Ctr Dr	702-9652